# THE T ZONE

The Path to Inner Power

# THE T ZONE

### The Path to Inner Power

## ALAN MESHER

BEACON CENTER PUBLICATIONS
SANTA MONICA, CALIFORNIA

ISBN 0-9660295-3-4

Cover design and typesetting: Carolyn F. Evans

First Edition: August 1997

**How to Order:**
Single copies may be ordered from:
Beacon Center Publications
2340 Ashland Avenue
Santa Monica, CA 90405
(310) 392-5105
E-mail: beaconprogram@ibm.net

To the people who inhabit the deep places in my heart –

Fran and Sam, Matthew and Mark

# TABLE OF CONTENTS

# ACKNOWLEDGEMENTS

The T Zone would never have come into being without the help of my good friend, the gifted visionary, Jackie Peters. She suggested I write this book and kept at me until I finished it. Lon Peterson listened as I developed many of my ideas and gave me timely insight and invaluable support. Special thanks to Rita Saiz, Philippe Benichou, Nora Stone and Belinda Derainieri for their editorial comments, encouragement and excitement about the material. I am indebted to David Shapiro and Mark Kalmansohn, my attorney, who both provided moral support and diverted me just enough during the making of The T Zone so that I was able to approach the daily task of writing with a clear mind.

I especially thank my son, Matthew, who is wise beyond his years, for understanding his dad's need to sit at his computer behind a closed door night after night and work on this book. When I see the goodness of my son and his friends I feel better about the future of the world.

No acknowledgement would be complete without mention of my dear friend Jackie Shaffer Fox who has been there in the good times and when the times were bleak. I thank her for her generosity and many acts of loving kindness.

# PREFACE

When I was a younger man, just graduated from college, I faced a difficult decision concerning my choice of a career. I had to decide between law school and a Ph.D. program, between a career as an attorney or one as a professor. The choice between these two professions was made more difficult by the fact that I wasn't really ready to choose either. I needed time off from academic life and intellectual studies to feel reconnected to my own life and grounded in the real world.

Instead of going off to graduate school I went off to a small town in southern New Hampshire to discover who I was and where I wanted to go with my life. My plan was to take a year off, get some time and distance with which to make a clear decision about my future, and then go on to either law school or graduate school.

As I got acquainted with the Monadnock region of southern New Hampshire, I kept hearing stories about an amazing woman named Eleanor Moore who had made a huge difference in the lives of many people in the area. If these stories were to be believed she was an extraordinarily gifted psychic and healer. The more accounts I heard about her the more fascinated I became. I knew I had to meet her. Finally, one evening a friend of mine announced he was going to see her. I didn't ask if I could accompany him, I just ran out and got in his car. As he climbed in the driver's seat, he looked at me strangely, and said nothing. A few minutes later we drove off down the dark highway to the town where she lived.

We were greeted at the front door by a small, rather round woman, with dark hair going gray, brown eyes gleaming with light, and a voice that seemed like silk on honey. She took my hands warmly in hers, introduced herself as Eleanor Moore and invited us into her home. After some small talk and a cup of tea we went into her study. Her eyes had a far away look to them as she first looked at me, then inside me and finally through me. It was an unnerving, awkward moment. But then the moment passed, she came back to her normal self and I breathed again. Eleanor smiled, her face lit up, and she started telling me about events from my childhood that no one else could have known about. The events she described were specific and accurate.

"The suffering and rejection you experienced as a child were necessary parts of your training and an important part of your development, even if you didn't know at the time that you were being trained for a special purpose," she went on. "Those of us who are here to do the Work must be sensitized to the sufferings of others. There is no other way to develop compassion but to have suffered yourself. Otherwise you will never understand the pain people carry. You have a warm and compassionate heart. What you went through has helped you."

As I sat there entranced, with my mouth agape, I became aware of an electrical force that seemed to be emanating from her. This force was flowing into me and as it continued to flow I found myself feeling more and more elated. Suddenly I felt something pop in my forehead and I became instantly aware of waves of brilliant color all around her. Those waves were gold and white, almost blinding in their brightness. As this power moved through my body my mood shifted in intensity from elation to ecstasy. Electrical currents were flowing from the soles of my feet to the top of my head and out through the top of my skull. Eleanor laughed as she observed my emotional state, then said softly to me, her voice filled with magic and music,

"You're right behind me. What I do, you'll do. Only you will take it further."

"Impossible!" I asserted. "I can't do what you do. I have no idea what this is, anyway. I don't have this kind of power. I can't make people feel wonderful or see hidden things, let alone see into their past and future. I have no psychic ability. I'm going to be a lawyer or a professor. That's why I went to college."

"You came to New Hampshire to find yourself," She said softly, her voice almost smiling. "It is no accident that you were lead to this place. This Work is your path. If you walk it you will find your destiny. But only you can choose to do so. Choose wisely."

I was unable to respond to her just then. My thought processes were overwhelmed by too much new data as well as inner conflict over old choices that were still unmade. I had no idea what the future held or where I was going. I was more confused than ever. The evening was soon over. That night I hardly slept. I tossed and turned for hours.

A few weeks later I was in her area and decided to drop in on her. She was busy with a number of clients but invited me to join her anyway. "I'm glad you're here," she said. "Your energy will be helpful in working on these people."

This time I didn't question her or protest. I sat down at her round table. A true master was at work. It was a privilege just to be there. Wisdom, power and love poured out of her. I drank it in. The people seated round the table laughed, cried and listened intently. Their faces softened and changed. Hurts and wounds were discharged. They left feeling much better, infused with light, love and hope. What I had witnessed was magic. I was hooked and I knew it. My future had just entered uncharted terrain. I had planned to stay one year and go on to grad school. I ended staying in New Hampshire three years, studying with Eleanor in an informal apprenticeship. Nothing was ever said about the terms of our arrangement. I was just over at her house as often as I could get there.

And so it was that my decision was made for me. I turned away from the conventional paths of law and teaching and chose instead the path less traveled and that, as the poet said, has made all the difference.

Over twenty-five years have passed since I met Eleanor Moore. She died in 1991. In that time I have worked with thousands of people. Each one of them has taught me something important and added to my fund of knowledge. I thank them all for the important contributions they have made to my life and work. The teachings and principles set forth in this volume are in no small measure the result of what I have learned from my clients. I hope you will find these teachings helpful as you walk forward down your path into the Light.

*There is nothing but water in holy pools,*
*I know, I have been swimming in them.*
*All the gods sculpted of wood and ivory can't say a word.*
*I know, I have been crying out to them.*
*The Sacred Books of the East are nothing but words.*
*I looked through their covers one day sideways.*
*What I talk about is only what I have lived through.*
*If you have not lived through something, it is not true.*

– KABIR

# CHAPTER ONE

## The Paradox of Life

A disturbing, inescapable paradox dwells in the heart of life. This problem defies resolution and makes life challenging and difficult. In the mental and spiritual realms of life mankind is blessed with unlimited potential. As a race we are capable of higher consciousness and inspired creativity. Our scientific discoveries and technological achievements continue to advance our standard of living. We have the capacity to enter mystical states of unity and oneness. We can touch God. But in our physical life we are saddled with crippling limitations. We are not immortal. Despite all our achievements life is short, difficult, and unfair. Time grinds us all down. We are born. One day we will die. What lies between is entirely up to us. That is all life guarantees. This bleak truth is the only real equality life provides.

Is life then as random and meaningless as it appears to be? Or has life been designed by a higher power to be difficult and uncertain for some unknown purpose that we fail to comprehend?

Life is meaningless only if we deny the reality of God. Without God there is neither a higher purpose to life nor any *linkage* between what we do here and what happens when we leave here. Without God any possible continuity between life and death is fiction, not fact: myth and fable, not truth and reality. If there is no ultimate reason for life, the quest for meaning and the search for enlightenment are simply the detours and delusions of a fool's path. If we believe that God does not exist then life is an accident, a mysterious aberration in a cold and sterile cosmos.

Unfortunately, the existence of God has not yet been proven scientifically. The absence of scientific proof is due to the fact that God is not a substance that can be quantified empirically and objectively. The experience of God is a subjective and personal one. God is felt, not measured. His existence is not just "out there", in interstellar space, but here, inside our hearts as well. The secret to proving the existence of God is internal and individual. We prove God exists one person at a time. *The reality of God does not yield to science. The mystery of God yields to love.*

If we can't find God in our hearts, we will not find Him outside of ourselves. If we can't feel Him in the internal world of our soul, we will not see Him working in the outer world of flesh and stone. One of the most important life tasks we will ever face is the challenge of transforming the unredeemed, dark parts of our psyche that hinder us from feeling the existence of God.

What prevents us from feeling the Oneness within is the personal suffering, anger and confusion we have not yet overcome. If the unhealed aspects of our psyche are holding us back is our failure to feel God's Presence our fault or His? God of course, does not need to prove himself to us. He already knows that he exists. But if he does exist we need to find Him to *complete* ourselves and *fulfill* our destiny.

### Why We Need God

We need to find the presence of God within ourselves because God represents the principle of Oneness. Oneness is not found in this world. It lies beyond. Spirituality is the search for the Oneness. Enlightenment is the direct and immediate experience of that Oneness. To experience the Oneness is to experience one's own Divine Nature and find God within. We hunger for the Oneness because it is the only thing in existence that will complete and fulfill us.

Nothing else will: Not love, power, money or fame.

The secret of a rich life is not found in the accumulation of tangible assets but in the realization of the intangible state of a higher consciousness that has reunited with the Oneness. When we touch the Oneness we know who we really are. This is because the Oneness contains our true identity, which is permanent and unchanging. All other forms of identity are limited, changeable and bound to physical existence. True identity transcends physical existence.

### God is Love

The great saints and mystics of all religions and spiritual traditions have spoken down the long corridor of time about their personal experiences of God. Most of these mystics never met or even heard of each other. They lived at different times in different parts of the world. In those distant eras there was no Internet, telephone, TV, radio or newspapers. There was no connection between them, no conspiratorial intent, no World Wide Web. Yet Buddha, Christ, Krishna and all the others said many similar things about their experience of God.

They each said God is Love and that the Divine experience is one of mercy, understanding, forgiveness and ecstasy. God represents the principle of Unity and Oneness. To touch the Oneness meant the end to all separation and suffering. Whenever these sages went inside themselves and touched *the bright place* where the Divine spark burned they felt the ecstasy and rapture of their connection to the Divine Source all over again. It was a flame that once lit would not, could not, go out.

A great teacher was once asked, "You are enlightened. Do you ever suffer?"

The teacher answered, "Only when I forget God." Suffering begins when our connection to the Oneness ends.

When these great sages were connected to the higher power they did not experience life as meaningless or random. They saw that life had a plan, a purpose and a reason. For them, Life was an opportunity to evolve toward the experience of Oneness. Since life held a Divine promise they realized, regardless of the suffering encountered and endured along the way, that life was a sacred experience.

### Life is a School

While life was sacred, it was also difficult and uncertain. In fact, life was a school we *chose* to enroll in *before* we came here so we might learn the many lessons needed to advance our consciousness. Several life lessons have a high degree of difficulty assigned to them. Some are very painful. A few seem unendurable. Others are delightful. No matter how much pain the learning of life lessons might cause, they must be encountered and overcome. Each lesson has an important contribution to make in the development of

consciousness. Every lesson is an important link in the evolutionary process and must be mastered before we can move
on to the next set of lessons.

### Responsibility and Free Will

These sages also saw that while we were given every
opportunity to master our life tasks and challenges, there
was no guarantee we would succeed at them. God gave
each of us free will and the innate ability to learn from the
challenges life presented to us. That is all. Our learning is
our responsibility. God has laid out the path. But we must
walk it. Our evolution, or our failure to evolve, is in our
hands. No one else is responsible.

The gift of free will adds a great deal of uncertainty to
life. The future is a large place. Nothing is set in stone.
Anything can happen. We never know where our choices
will lead or how our lives will unfold. Life is a risky and
uncertain business.

The one thing for certain in all this uncertainty is that
what happens between birth and death is up to us. Will we
take advantage of our opportunities to grow or will we be
stubborn and persist in denial and suffering? Will we make
the right choices? Will we evolve and move closer to God?
Or will we instead turn away from the deepest needs of our
psyche? It is all up to us.

## The Power of Right Action

Since we have free will we can choose to do the right thing and act in our best interest or we can choose to do the wrong thing and act contrary to our highest good. If we do the right thing we will evolve more rapidly. If we do the wrong thing, such as intentionally harming another person out of malice, roadblocks are automatically placed along our path. Free will does not occur in isolation. Every action causes a reaction. We are never free of the consequences of those actions. If there are roadblocks in our life they are there because we put them there through past wrong actions. Since there are always consequences to our actions it is the wise person who does the right thing. When we knowingly do the wrong thing we sabotage ourselves.

## Momentum and Consequences

Right action creates positive momentum narrowing the gap between where we are, and the other shore of consciousness, where God is waiting. Right action quickens the evolutionary process. Bad choices, on the other hand, create bad situations. Negative actions eventually lead to inertia and stagnation. They prohibit forward movement and insure that we will fall behind in the quest for consciousness. If we continue down the path of wrong action the path of hope disappears into the thick mists of time. By choosing the negative path we choose, no matter how unconscious that choice may be, to widen the gap between mind and soul, leaving us more alone and separate than ever before. Negative action, or evil is a toxic force that fragments our psyche, and creates dark holes in our soul. Rather than evolve we regress.

The fact that evil has serious negative consequences makes it inevitable that our potential for growth will be severely curtailed if we choose to follow the negative path. Those consequences may stretch beyond the scope of this lifetime and negatively influence several lifetimes to come.

The harvest of the bad karma that we have sown will have to be cleaned up. It may take many lifetimes for all those bad seeds to germinate and many more before all the consequences of those actions have been rooted out of our psyche. To choose the path of evil is to fail at the purpose of life. The fruit of that failure is more pain and suffering over a longer period of time. The path of evil is a fool's game.

## Why We Are Not Victims

Because we have free will we are never victims. We choose our own destiny, either consciously or unconsciously. If we continue to make the wrong choices evolution becomes a much more formidable and difficult task than need be. By making the wrong choices we enlarge the gap between where we are and where our fulfillment and joy is. That gap is not static. It increases with every bad choice and every evil or negative action. The distance between where we are and where God is lies in our hands.

### The Principle of Duality

Spirituality is the search for Oneness. The world we live in however, is ruled by the Principle of Duality. In duality everything is split and fragmented. Humanity is split into male and female. The day is split into night and day. Electricity is split into two poles, positive and negative. Life occurs between the poles of birth and death.

The tension between the positive and negative poles of duality generates the energy of life. What we then experience is the result of the dynamic movement of energy between the poles of existence. Without duality there would be no movement. Life would be static. Little would happen.

The movement of energy flowing back and forth between the poles of existence creates constant change, giving us new opportunities for growth. A Duality System is dynamic *and* unstable. Uncertainty is its only constant. For several reasons it is the perfect environment for the evolution of consciousness. First, nothing is certain. Second, we have free will. Third, we have to make choices. Fourth, our growth or lack of growth is determined by our choices. We control our destiny. We are not victims.

### The Wounded Psyche

Everyone who enters through the birth gate into the Duality System of this planet enters with wounds in their soul that they need to heal. These wounds have fragmented our psyches and separated us from experiencing and knowing the Oneness of life. These psychic wounds are our karma. They have created the gaps in our being that separate us from fulfillment and joy. Until we heal these gaps they control our lives, create more pain and suffering, and keep us from finding the God within.

We are bound to this Duality System until we heal our wounds and restore our psyches to the Oneness. Our true life task is to move closer to God. We are here to close the gaps in our being, not widen and extend them. Whether or not we accomplish this task is up to us. In a Duality System there is always doubt and uncertainty. That is because in a Duality System the presence of the Principle of Unity and Oneness is not obvious and apparent. In a Duality System everything that is not obvious is doubted. God, for example, may or may not exist. It is up to us to find him. That is the nature of the Great Game of life. Everything depends on us.

The Duality System of the world may never change. But the duality and separateness within each of us must certainly change. That is the main assignment and challenge of the human experience. Conventional psychotherapy gives us insight into the problems lurking in the unconscious and strategies and medications to deal with them. While that kind of approach is often beneficial, it is not enough. Gaining insight into our problems and learning to cope with them does not close the gaps in our psyches, end our suffering or lead us into the experience of the Oneness. *Information is not transformation.* We need to transform our inner gaps, not just cope with them and medicate ourselves from feeling our pain.

### Why Life is Difficult and Uncertain

Life is *uncertain* because in a Duality System the only constant is constant change. Human beings crave stability, but a duality system is inherently unstable and unpredictable. We never really know what will happen.

Life is *difficult* because we all have gaps in our psyches that separate us from the Oneness. Without access to the Oneness we don't know who we really are. Our true identity is a mystery. The disconnection from the Oneness is the source of all suffering. There is no access to the Oneness without the transformation of our nature. Any attempt to close the gap short of the transformation required will result in this message flashing on the silent screen of our soul, "Access Denied. Go back. You are not ready for the Oneness. You have major work to do on yourself."

Life then, is not random and meaningless. It is deliberate and intentional. We are in these bodies and on this planet for a very important and profound reason. However, we will never know how precious life is until we are reconnected to the Divine Presence. God lives inside each of us. Our task is to find him. The good news is God does not discriminate. He has no favorites. He is an equal opportunity employer who wants everyone to work for Him. If we work for Him, He will work for us.

What is critical in life is not the movement between the opposites or the fluctuations in our circumstances but what we can learn from our experience and our time on this planet. It is the growth we make, not the prizes, honors or riches we might be fortunate enough to win that determines the true value of our life. In the end the only thing we can take with us from this life is our growth. Everything else remains behind. And when we are born again the only thing that will return with us is the growth we made, or failed to make, in this lifetime.

# CHAPTER TWO

## Evolution

*It is so much more . . . convincing to see all the things that happen to me than to observe how I make them happen. Indeed, the animal nature of man makes him resist seeing himself as the maker of his circumstances.*

– CARL JUNG

*Psychology and Religion: West and East,* Vol. 11 of the Collected Works of C.G. Jung

Life is difficult because we do not have the consciousness to be at peace with uncertainty. All higher consciousness depends on the integration and wholeness of the psyche. Inner Peace is the result of that integration. Thus, the path to peace leads by necessity through the unfinished business (trauma/karma) secreted away in our soul. The unresolved material entrenched in the unconscious fragments the psyche and causes unhappiness.

Neurosis is never peaceful. Rather, it is internally turbulent and violent, the result of a constant clash between anxiety and fear. Everyone has trauma somewhere, embedded in subtle layers of mind and soul. Healing that trauma is the major reason we choose to come to the physical environment. As we heal the wounds and unresolved issues in our psyche we evolve out of our personal neuroses toward the divine light within.

Evolution then, is the movement of consciousness from the state of fragmentation toward a higher state of Oneness, from the strictly personal to the impersonal and universal. To reach the Oneness we must explore and conquer our darkness. Thus, we go up into the Light by going down into our personal Darkness. We experience impersonal reality by overcoming the splits and schisms in our personal reality. When we heal ourselves of the fear of life and the need to control our personal reality we can let go and let God enter our lives.

Until we attain the Oneness we are in a prison of our

own making. We are both the jailer and the prisoner. We cannot set ourselves free until we choose to heal ourselves. We determine the length of our sentence by choosing either to engage our karma or let that karma dominate our future. If we decide to engage the negative or shadow side of our nature our sentence may be commuted in fairly short order. If we choose to evade and deny the reality of unresolved, painful material in our unconscious that confinement may be a life sentence or a sentence lasting lifetimes.

The metaphysical principle that controls the quality of our life experience is simply this; *the negative elements of the psyche will prevail until we confront and heal them.* This principle cannot be gotten around no matter how clever or manipulative we might be in trying to defeat it. It is not subject to emotional appeal, no matter how fervent or sincere our plea may be. We can fool and convince ourselves of almost anything. The mind is a gifted deceiver. We can never fool God. The higher law that watches over us is absolutely impartial. It treats everyone exactly the same.

If we are here in a physical body we have work to do to make ourselves psychically whole and conscious. That work is the true purpose of the physical plane. Basically, we are all incomplete, works of art that are unfinished. We are here to finish the sculpting process. We would not *have* to be here otherwise. A Duality System such as the earth is primarily a growth environment. We take on a physical body so we can be in the environment that offers the greatest potential to provoke our negative side, and force our growth. It is the essential need to grow that makes life difficult. We grow by overcoming the internal obstacles in our psyche. When we overcome those obstacles the roadblocks are lifted from our path and the evolutionary process is ignited. The sculpting process is complete when we achieve enlightenment.

## Enlightenment

Enlightenment is simply another name for normalcy and sanity. The enlightened person has resolved his psychic splits and emotional fragmentation. His inner darkness has been transformed into spiritual light. That light is the basis for his conscious connection to the Oneness. If he had not first gone through the process of redeeming his darkness and recovering his light that enlightenment would not be possible.

## The Psyche's Buried Treasure

Spiritual evolution *depends* on making the choice to confront the negative side of our psyche. As I have said before, that confrontation is the basis of all true growth. The negative side of our psyche is where we hide our buried treasure. Buried treasure is what our unconscious pain and suffering really is. When we raise it up to consciousness and heal it, it is no longer negative, fragmenting, destructive or heavy. When we raise up and heal this buried treasure it is no longer hostile and antagonistic to our conscious goals and intentions. Instead it is reintegrated into our psyche as lessons we have learned. Trauma that has been overcome is no longer a cause of suffering but a source of wisdom. It makes us more powerful because it closes the gaps in our being. Turning psychic darkness into spiritual light is the basis of all spiritual evolution and the essential task of the transformation process. We find the fuel we need to climb higher on the evolutionary highway in the negative regions of the unconscious. *Mining the Negative* is a fruitful endeavor that leads to higher consciousness.

### The Internal War

The choice to pursue conscious confrontation as the only viable path to wholeness and accelerated evolution intensifies the internal war between the light and dark elements in the psyche. The process of conscious confrontation forces us to look at what is healed and true about us, and what is unhealed and only rationalized within us. It compels us to choose between accepting responsibility for our actions so we might change ourselves, and assigning blame to others for our deeds so we need not face ourselves.

Conscious confrontation with the dark side of the unconscious demands that we choose between the ability to love and heal on the one hand, and the need to control and wound on the other. Finally, the process requires that we choose who our ultimate master will be, the soul or the ego. In this high stakes encounter everything rides on our capacity to make the right choice. The quality of our life and the evolution of our soul hang in the balance.

## The Internal War of Overcoming

What are the alternatives to mining the negative? If we choose to do nothing, and not engage ourselves in the internal war of overcoming, we will lose by default. No matter what we might achieve in the external world, our internal life, our *real* life, will be an exercise in futility.

Elvis Presley is a case in point. He achieved great fame and experienced tremendous adulation from his fans but on the inside he was sad, lonely and lost. He felt an inner call to minister to his fellow man but ignored his inner voice and turned instead to drugs to medicate himself from his pain. But drugs and being on stage could never keep the pain away for very long. It always came back. It always does.

Elvis was not only young and rich when he died but also lost and unfulfilled. He couldn't take his fame and riches with him when he went but he did take his sadness, loneliness and pain. His failure to reach for inner fulfillment was etched deeply on his soul. In life he did nothing to close the gaps in his being. Instead his choice to do drugs deepened the tears in his psyche. Undoubtedly, the soul we knew as Elvis will return to the physical environment in a different personality to take up the challenge of growth once more.

Elvis's tragic end illustrates an important life principle. The choices we make define us. It is up to us to define ourselves in ways that serve our soul rather than deepen our emotional wounds.

A worse choice than doing nothing is to consciously choose to do evil. If we choose the path of evil we will certainly lose in the game of life. The pursuit of temporary power and the fleeting fulfillment of desire at any cost is the path to long term destruction. If we deliberately and intentionally inflict pain on others we inflict the same or worse pain on ourselves. It might take a little longer to catch up with us, that's all. Don't let time fool you. The fruit of our actions will find us. What was once sweet will become bitter. The doer and the deed are intimately connected.

Richard Nixon rose to the presidency of the United States by destroying the good reputation and character of many of his opponents. It wasn't until he had reached the zenith of his power that his karma found him and brought him down. His actions during the Watergate crisis destroyed his reputation and tarnished his legacy. He was forced to resign the Presidency in disgrace. He may have been criminally prosecuted for his actions if not pardoned by his successor, President Ford. No less ardent a Republican than former Sen. Barry Goldwater, himself the Republican Presidential candidate in 1964, called former President Nixon "a thief and a liar." When you fall from a high place, you fall fast and hard.

The third choice we can make is to confront the dark side of ourselves. Choosing this path means we have a chance to win in the game of life. It is the only sane choice we have. Besides the certainty of death, all life grants us is a *chance* to grow. While death is certain, growth is not. If we don't make the right choices we won't grow.

### The Horizontal Scale

In life we all have to deal with two scales of accomplishment. The first scale is the horizontal one. The horizontal scale is the material scale. It deals with what we have or don't have and how we feel about ourselves as a result of our external success or lack thereof. On the left end of the scale is survival. On the right end is success. When we are stuck in survival mode, anxiety and stress are the dominant notes of our experience.

Survival is about lack, both materially and emotionally. It is never about abundance. In the survival mode there is always the fear of not having enough. On the psychological level this fear translates into low self-esteem. In survival mode one lives in chronic fear, confusion and powerlessness.

### Survival Consciousness and the Victim Mentality

Most people that are stuck in survival mode have chosen to be a victim. This choice may be a conscious or an unconscious one. It doesn't really matter. The result is the same. A victim is someone who has given away his power and feels isolated, alienated and alone as a result. It is the surrender of one's power that creates the victim mentality.

When a victim gives away his power he experiences a great deal of anger. That anger is his emotional response to the imploding chain reaction now occurring in his psyche. By relinquishing his power he has thrown the delicate balance of his psyche out of operational integrity, and shattered his self-esteem as well. What remains is rage. It is the victim's last weapon and only defense against the fear and terror he feels at the core of his soul.

### The Victims Loss of Personal Power and Self Esteem

The victim now lacks the power he needs to move forward in his life and has lost what measure of self-esteem he may have once possessed. He has given these things away by not establishing healthy psychological boundaries. Without strong boundaries he is easy prey to those who are always on the lookout for weak people to manipulate and exploit. The victimization process usually begins early in childhood when a child's emotional and psychological needs are not met by his parents. Abusive and emotionally neglectful parents destroy their child's self-esteem before it has a chance to form. A child having to cope with angry and abusive parents learns early that it is dangerous to stand up for himself. As a result he may spend the rest of his life shrinking from conflict or conversely, seeking it out, only to get beaten down time and time again. In either case the result is the same. The sense of powerlessness is continually reinforced.

### Rationalization is Not Reality

As a result of the negative imprinting on his psyche during childhood the victim has been defeated before he had a chance to find his way in life. The sun has set in his soul before it was given the chance to rise. His psyche has become a dark wasteland where nothing but weeds grow. All that remains is a large gap of futility, a parched inner desert that has disconnected him from his inner source where he could drink from the fountain of life and find his real potential. In surrendering his power the victim becomes an emotional cripple, separated from the light inside him. The best he can now do, as long as he chooses to stay locked in his rage and do nothing is to endure and survive. That's no life at all, but it's the life lead by many. Since this situation is painful and destructive those stuck in the victim role often attempt to convince themselves that they are doing the best they can. *Rationalization, however, is not reality*. It's what we do when we can't get what we need or fail to stand up for ourselves.

### Rage and the Victim Mentality

The victim of course, feels justified in his rage. "After all," he thinks. "Look what happened to me. Look what they did to me." This tendency toward self-justification can make him stubborn and difficult to deal with. On an unconscious level the victim believes that his rage is all he has left. If he were to surrender it he would lose the little dignity that remains. His psychological state is dominated by fear, anger and powerless. His rage binds him to the victim role. This negative emotional profile creates a reality context that can be hard to overcome.

## How a Reality Context Works

A reality context works this way. If you believe that you will never be able to have what you want because someone did something to you when you were a child and made you a victim then your adult experience will conform to the belief you formed in childhood. Belief shapes experience.

A client of mine had a mother who terrorized her psychologically and physically beat her. Her father sexually molested her when she was little. She was robbed of her self-esteem before it had a chance to form and became a victim before she knew she had personal power. As an adult all her relationships were with men who abused her and were emotionally cold and distant. She is finally tired of being the victim and wants to do something about it.

The question facing her is if she has the requisite courage to face her pain; then to feel her pain; and finally heal her pain. Overcoming intense psychic suffering can be easier to achieve than you might think. Don't let your mind imprison you with its fears. Those fearful thoughts and images are a diversion. Their purpose is to keep you bound and chained where you are, thereby preventing you from moving forward. The truth is that it is far easier to heal than to remain unhealed. Unconscious pain is more painful and destructive than the pain you are finally willing to face. Lao Tzu, the great Chinese Sage and founder of Taoism said regarding this point, "Because the sage confronts his difficulties he never experiences them." The opposite of this statement is also true. If we don't confront the pain inside us we will continually re-experience our problems.

*We attract to ourselves whatever energy is inside us. The life we experience is the version of reality that is imbedded in our unconscious. We live out what we unconsciously believe to be true about ourselves. In this sense, life is a self-fulfilling prophecy.*

### Progress on the Horizontal Scale

On the horizontal scale the way we progress from survival to success is by improving our self-image and erecting a new belief system to create a different experience in reality. If we feel good about ourselves and worthy of having what we want it is far easier to attract positive things to us.

I know of a case where a woman wanted a relationship with a wealthy man. She went on retreat in a mountainous area of the Midwest for two weeks. The area was largely uninhabited. She spent her time alone writing affirmations about what she wanted, visualizing the result she wished to achieve, and meditating on attracting a very rich man into her life. Shortly after she returned home she met an extremely wealthy man who eventually built her a large home and took her travelling with him all over the world.

The only problem was that while she was relatively young he was in his late seventies. He had plenty of money but I don't believe that he was exactly the companion of her dreams.

This woman effected powerful change in her life by consciously creating a new belief about herself and then getting her subconscious to accept it as true. She succeeded in restructuring her subconscious context. Her external situation then shifted to accommodate her new reality system. On the horizontal scale visualization, affirmation, breathwork and meditation are powerful tools for retraining the subconscious reality system. These tools can help us move from a survival state toward a more successful life experience. Indeed, various programs that exploit and combine different elements of these tools have been big sellers in the marketplace for many years.

## Achieving Material Success

For the last several hundred years Western society has been preoccupied with creating material success. In the West we equate material success with happiness and fulfillment. But people who become successful often realize that success and happiness do not necessarily coincide. Attaining the one does not guarantee the other.

A client of mine once told me a story. A friend of hers had seen a psychiatrist regularly for years. One day she asked the doctor a question. "Dr." she said. "Would you rather have a rich client or a poor one?"

"A rich one," he replied without hesitation.

"Just as I figured he'd respond." She thought to herself. "He's only after the money." Then she asked the Dr. another question. "Why would you rather have the rich client?" The answer seemed pretty obvious but she thought she'd ask it anyway.

The Dr. replied promptly. "Because the rich client already knows that money and success won't make him happy. The poor man still suffers from that illusion."

"Oh?" She replied, thrown off balance by her cynicism towards the doctor's motives. "I hadn't thought of that."

If we could ask the lady who changed her belief system and landed a wealthy man if she was now emotionally fulfilled and psychologically free or had she simply changed and rearranged her external situation I wonder what her response would be. Success is one thing, fulfillment and joy another. They can coincide, but only when we do the inner work necessary to heal our wounds, not just cover them over with a new belief system and a method for creating success. If that is all we are doing then success is merely an opiate, another form of addiction.

## Desire and the Horizontal Scale

We must realize at some point that getting what we want is not getting who we are. The horizontal scale functions under the control of desire. The key thing to know about desire is that it constantly tricks us into thinking that if I only had "this" (whatever "this" may be for you) I would be happy. Desire is seductive, leading us to believe that whatever we may need to complete ourselves and find happiness exists outside ourselves. While we are ruled by Desire we never look within. The answer to unhappiness is always what "I need or I want," never what "I am".

## Desire and Disconnection

Desire is the result of our primal disconnection from the Oneness. The powerful cravings desire produces in us are desperate attempts to find a replacement for the loss of that higher connection. Without that union we are not only not whole, we are also unconscious. Desire flourishes in a psychic system that is *disconnected* from higher truth and *unconscious* of that loss. The truth is nothing can replace that loss except *reunion* with the Higher Self. Unchecked, unconscious desire is a powerful force that as it progresses leads to addiction, powerlessness, and codependent relationships. Desire inevitably widens the gaps in our psyche.

## Planet Earth as a Psychic Hospital

Planet earth is the place we all have to come to, to repair the various and sundry gaps in our psyche and move forward on our path towards *reunion* with the Divine Presence or Oneness. The earth is not a place of light and truth. Rather, it is an environment lacking light and truth. We all have come here to rectify and overcome the tears in our psyche, not to perpetuate and enlarge them. We overcome what is missing in our life by finding the answer to wholeness in ourselves, not by falling into the web desire weaves so well.

## The Importance of Critical Mass

Only when enough of us rediscover our conscious connection to the Oneness will this planet become a place of light and truth. The stakes in the evolutionary battle for the future are very high. Desire, like the duality system it exists in, creates instability and uncertainty. These two forces, fitting fiercely together like the iron hand in the iron glove, have created a difficult set of circumstances to overcome. Their combined intention is to keep us from the path of evolution and self-mastery. The overcoming of these forces is the key to the rediscovery of the Oneness within us.

Nothing is guaranteed in the battle for control over our psyche. Nor is anything worth winning won easily. Evolution requires a conscious and diligent struggle with the dark forces hidden in the psyche. It is a serious matter of grave consequence. Very few comprehend just how high are the stakes in this battle. Rather than having the time to focus on our true purpose we get swept off course all too easily by the problems of daily living. Our attention shifts elsewhere. We forget that our future is in our hands right now. So too, is the future of this planet. Life will be what we choose to make of it. Nothing is accidental.

### Desire and Maya

In Eastern philosophy desire is the unconscious power that traps us in "maya" or illusion. This trap, as long as we allow ourselves to be subject to it, keeps us bound to the horizontal scale, where we can get what we want, but never discover who we really are. Fulfillment does not come from our assets. It comes from our awareness. The task of creating more consciousness and awareness is the work of the other major scale of life, the vertical scale.

### The Vertical Scale

Until recently the vertical scale has been largely ignored in the West. Instead, the West has focussed on raising the material standard of living. Now that affluence is much more widespread millions of people are waking up and realizing that material success is not enough. It has not made them happy nor provided a solution to the problem of life. Comfort and security are important and necessary, but they are not sufficient to solve the problem of inner fulfillment.

The vertical scale is the scale of mind and conscious-ness. It is the internal scale of depth and truth. Its main focus is spiritual evolution. On the bottom, or southern end, of the vertical scale is the Ego and Personality. On the northern end of the scale is Soul and Spirit. The task of the vertical scale is to free the mind from its enslavement to the ego and connect it to the Soul and then the Spirit.

## Soul and Spirit

There is an important distinction that we should make at the outset between the Soul and the Spirit. The spirit is the highest aspect of us. It is the part of us that lives in the Oneness. It always has. It always will. It is our North Star. It guides us on our journey home from afar.

The Soul, on the other hand, is the part of us that is *evolving* towards the Oneness. As we grow and develop from one life to the next it grows with us. The soul stores the records of what we have learned and overcome, and what we still have to learn and overcome. It carries forward from one lifetime to the next the talents we have developed and the wisdom we have gained from our past experience. It also bears forward from one lifetime to the next the trauma and pain we have suffered and been unable to process through, complete and heal.

The soul registers our growth toward the Oneness as well as the areas of our experience that are still bound to pain and suffering. These unresolved areas of consciousness need to be completed if we are to continue to grow and move forward in our evolution. Until we heal them, they hold us back. The soul carries the records of where we are conscious and where we remain unconscious; where we have found resolution and where we have yet to find resolution. The soul is not perfect, fixed and complete. It is a dynamic, changing organism containing a mixture of wisdom and suffering, good and bad, light and dark. Our task is to help it move forward toward re-union with the Spirit. When that task is accomplished it will help us be part of the Oneness as well.

For example, if we have acted in ways that are detrimental to the well being of other people in another lifetime the soul will carry forward the impact those actions have on us into the future of that lifetime, or if necessary, into future lifetimes. As we stated in the previous chapter, nothing happens in a vacuum. Actions have consequences. When we behave in a harmful manner we create a future roadblock that will delay our growth and cause us suffering. When we do encounter that roadblock we will experience the other side of our actions. This time, we will be cast as the victim, not the perpetrator, in the play of life. The purpose of the play is to educate us in ways that serve our growth. The suffering we experience as a result of the change in our role is designed to sensitize us to the pain that harmful actions can cause.

### The Soul and Change

The soul then, is not an immutable, unchanging part of our psyche. The soul is subject to growth and change. As we heal ourselves the soul gathers more internal light and sheds the darkness it has outgrown. Souls have a growth cycle that parallels the stages of life in the physical world; Infant, baby, young, mature and old. What differentiates soul age is not intelligence, but attitude and understanding. As a soul matures it tends to become more tolerant, accepting and understanding. Through long cycles of suffering it learns sensitivity and compassion. Through many experiences in the earth plane it learns that focusing on self and one's own success is not enough, that power and control do not fulfill, and finally, that wisdom lies in letting go and loving unconditionally.

### The Reunion of Soul and Spirit

When the energies of the soul have been fully resolved and the lessons of self-development have been fully mastered the internal soul light becomes very bright. That light is highly magnetic and powerful. It draws to it the higher light of the Spirit that has been watching the soul's development from afar. Light attracts light. The spirit will keep its distance from the soul until all the darkness and unresolved trauma in the psyche have been transformed and overcome. When the soul is clear and only light remains the spirit comes, not before. Then and only then will the reunion of soul and spirit occur and the person become fully conscious once more, reunited with the Oneness.

Until that moment the person is still bound to some extent to the challenges of the vertical scale. He cannot escape until he closes the gaps in his being and makes himself whole. The reunion of soul and spirit is enlightenment. In that instant we are reconnected to the Oneness and become fully conscious.

Before the soul is reunited to the spirit it must go through all the necessary stages of growth from the fear and terror of the infant soul to the narcissism, competitiveness and belief that success is all there is of the young soul. Gradually over many cycles of experience and difficult lessons the soul becomes group conscious, developing sensitivity, empathy and compassion as it moves up the vertical scale toward reunion with the Oneness.

As the soul becomes established in its old soul perception it realizes that to truly succeed we must all succeed; that there is nothing as uplifting as helping others. Moreover, it realizes that one of the most direct ways to accelerate our movement toward the oneness is through serving others.

### The Path of Service

The path of Service should never be self-sacrificing. Instead it should be self-fulfilling. We serve because we feel better for doing the act of service. The giving of love to others fills us with unconditional love from the Oneness. When we serve others we become a channel for the Oneness to flow through us. What we give is given back to us in greater abundance. Unconditional love is a powerful form of healing for the psyche. It repairs the gaps in the inner self. Service is a natural high. Group consciousness, sensitivity, empathy, compassion and service are all qualities that blossom in the late mature and old soul cycles. These qualities are the foundation for the enlightenment experience.

## Enlightenment

From the elevated perspective of the Spirit enlightenment is not something beyond the normal but rather a return to the normal. It is not the exception, but the rule. On the higher planes of consciousness it is normal and expected to be connected to the Oneness. We are not allowed in these environs without that connection. It is the *sine qua non* that opens the gate to the higher heavens. Neither money nor power nor fame will open that gate. Worldly success is no guarantor of inner freedom. Only here on earth, does it seem normal and accepted to be disconnected from the Oneness.

The soul of someone in the young soul cycle will not be able to reach the same level of spiritual brightness as the soul of someone in the old soul cycle. The reason for the differing degree of spiritual potential between the soul levels is that the older soul has had much more experience, learned many more lessons, and gone farther in the evolutionary process. Inner Light is developed through the learning process. Because of its advantage in the learning process (it has been in the earth environment longer) it is more prepared to adjust to the higher light of the Spirit.

In terms of evolution we are never given more than we can handle. Experience counts. The young soul might want enlightenment but would not achieve it until all the internal conditions have been met. These include mastering all the necessary lessons for growth and resolving the hidden trauma in his psyche. Each of the five stages of the soul's maturation process from baby through infant, young and mature, to old has specific growth lessons that apply to that stage of the soul's development. We will stay at each level until we master all the lessons that apply to that stage. Sometimes we spend many lives in each level. Evolution is a long process. We can only go as far as the potential of our soul age allows us to. The young soul's potential for spiritual growth is more limited than that of the older soul because he has more to learn and farther to go on the vertical scale.

This type of distinction is not applicable on the horizontal scale. Success does not discriminate in the same way enlightenment does. It is not based on merit or determined by soul age. Anyone can achieve success. Not everyone can achieve enlightenment. But everyone can quicken their growth and find their appropriate level of wholeness and fulfillment. The more we choose to pursue our wholeness the faster we accelerate our movement toward the Oneness. The closer we get to the moment of reunion the more light we carry in our body and psyche. That light confers happiness, fulfillment and success. Once we have it life becomes much sweeter.

Finding the sweetness and joy in life is the task of the vertical scale. Often, we have to wage a war against the dark side of ourselves to attain that sweetness. We activate the vertical scale by choosing to confront ourselves and face the hidden side of our nature. We are usually terrified to face that side of us thinking that we will find out all sorts of terrible things about ourselves that are permanent and true and cannot be corrected. If we do have the courage to overcome our fear what we will find is a rotting storehouse of false beliefs that are lies about ourselves. In making the vertical ascent we take back the power we have ceded away to fear and false belief. It takes all of our power to reach the Oneness. Abraham Lincoln once wrote, "A house divided against itself cannot stand." As long as our psyche is split we cannot stand in our power and make the vertical ascent.

All of us have to face the two scales of life, the search for fulfillment and the search for success. Join them together and they form the Cross of Life. Everyone has to bear that cross. There are no exceptions. The purpose of life on this planet is to grow and evolve.

# CHAPTER THREE

## Confrontation with the Unconscious

*If the wrong man uses the right means, the right means work in the wrong way.*

— THE SECRET OF THE GOLDEN FLOWER

Confrontation with the negative, unconscious side of our nature is the foundation of the vertical ascent. Without that confrontation there is no ascent. If we don't face ourselves we can't move forward.

## The Positive Gate of the Spiritual Path

Most people who set foot on the spiritual path enter it from the positive gate, where spirituality seems safe, serene, and comforting. The positive gate of spirituality includes practices such as Yoga, Tai Chi, meditation, creative visualization, breathing exercises, prayer, and affirmation. These practices are beneficial. They relieve stress, calm the nervous system, build positive energy, and enhance health and well being. But they do not transform consciousness. Instead the practices of the positive gate often keep us from connecting with our buried trauma by enabling us to rise above our pain. In this sense, the practices of the positive gate are a form of medication. While empowering us on the surface, conscious level, they disempower us on the deeper subconscious level. As they help us feel better about ourselves, they separate us further from our pain. They do not transform that pain; they simply bury it more deeply, in hidden crevices of the unconscious. From this perspective, pursuing the practices of the positive gate without balancing them by pursuing the practice of confrontation with our buried trauma can actually widen the gaps in our psyche.

Carl Jung, the great psychologist, commented on this problem in a 1936 journal article titled, "Yoga and the West." "Yoga," he wrote. "Means . . . the final detachment of consciousness from all bondage to object and subject. But since one cannot detach oneself from something of which one is unconscious, the European must first learn to know his subject. This, in the West, is what one calls the unconscious. Yoga technique applies itself exclusively to the conscious mind and will. Such an undertaking promises success only when the unconscious has no potential worth mentioning, that is to say, when it does not contain large portions of the personality. If it does, then all conscious effort remains futile, and what comes out of this cramped condition is a caricature or even the exact opposite of the intended result."

The practices of the positive gate can be highly seductive. They wrap the comforting illusion around us that we are transforming ourselves by following these practices. These exercises work like medication works. They provide a sense of well being as long as we practice them, just as a drug will suppress our symptoms as long as we ingest it. But when we stop taking our medication or discontinue these practices on a regular basis the old problems quickly reappear.

The truth is we can stay airborne and in denial only so long before reality sets in. Sooner or later we will fall back down to ground zero and re-experience the emotional pain buried in our bodies. That pain didn't disappear. It wasn't magically transformed, only anesthetized. Even in a Duality System geared to change and uncertainty one truth is constant. We never escape ourselves. But we can waste lots of time, even whole lifetimes that would be better spent pursuing a real and lasting transformation.

## Physics and Consciousness

Earlier in the twentieth century physicists performed an important experiment. They bombarded an atom with energy to learn what would happen to the atom. What they observed in their experiment was that the electrons of the bombarded atom absorbed the extra energy. As these electrons absorbed the additional power they shifted into more elevated orbits, spinning around the nucleus at significantly higher speeds. After the electrons burned up the excess energy they returned to their base orbit, rotating once again at their normal speed.

The impact the energy had on the atom was *temporary*, just as the impact that the practices of the positive gate have is also temporary if we have not first made the vertical ascent. There was no fundamental change. The truth is that the positive gate of spirituality is much more powerful and positive as a force in our evolution if we make the vertical ascent first. In the spiritual journey the old adage is always true. "First things first."

## Meditation and Transformation

Some years ago I remember reading the story of a meditator who had spent large periods of time attending meditation retreats in Europe. These retreats brought hundreds of people together for group meditation and the practice of Hatha Yoga. During these gatherings many people had extremely powerful experiences on higher planes of consciousness. The group energy created during these events was intoxicating and addicting. Virtually everyone who attended participated in the spiritual high created by the group energy.

When this man returned home the energy high he experienced finally wore off and he realized that despite his spiritual experiences nothing had changed. He was still the same person with the same problems, fears and neuroses. He realized then that meditation and yoga could not answer his need for transformation. His experience taught him that consciousness is transformed by transforming ground zero, not by attempting to rise above it. By turning back to face our pain we can overcome it. If we choose to avoid that confrontation, looking away from our pain or ahead into the future, we are actually keeping that pain alive and feeding it with our denial. The future will be a harder place to live in and to find the fulfillment that is so elusive to so many because we haven't resolved our past.

## Consciousness as a Circle

Let us assume for a moment that our consciousness is like a circle. Part of that circle is clear and white, some is gray and some is black. The gray, clear and dark areas can be arranged any way you wish, and given whatever percentage of the available area inside the circle you choose. The circle for example could be divided into thirds, or the three areas could be separated randomly or haphazardly.

There could be a rational design or a chaotic breakdown. It doesn't really matter.

The clear or white areas represent the resolved, positive, strong areas of the psyche. The gray areas represent confusion, uncertainty, low self-esteem and sadness. The black areas indicate buried trauma and contain highly charged negative emotions such as depression, rage, terror, resentment and hatred. Virtually all of us have all three domains in our psyche. A few of us are mostly clear, while most of us have a preponderance of energy in the gray and black domains.

It is only natural that we try to live in the white zone of the psyche where we feel clear and strong. This is the area in which we have resolved certain of our issues, learned from past experience and taken back our power. It is the part of us that we have re-integrated. The practices of the positive gate are attempts to both center ourselves in that zone and remain there as long as possible. If we can prolong our time in the white zone life feels safer and more satisfying. Lingering in the white zone, however, does not change ground zero or transform us in any meaningful way. It just makes us complacent and deluded. To move forward in our evolution we must step outside the comfort zone and make contact with the gray and dark areas of our psyche.

## Stepping Beyond the Comfort Zone

As we have stated previously, making contact with the

shadow side of the psyche is the first step we must take in the battle to reclaim our power from the ways it has been fragmented and sealed off in our bodies. The negative emotions buried in the body are the result of past trauma we have experienced. These unexpressed emotions represent the part of our life energy that has been split off and is now unavailable to us. Every traumatic event that results in more fragmentation of our life energy robs us of another piece of our personal power. The purpose of stepping beyond the comfort zone is to reclaim our power and integrate our psyche. It takes *all* of our power to make the vertical ascent and evolve. **Confrontation is exploration.** Evolution demands that we set off from our snug perch and explore the hidden continents of the unconscious psyche. The white zone is not our destination. It is simply the place we must embark from.

T.S. Eliot stated this idea very succinctly in his collection of poems, *The Four Quartets*, when he wrote the following verse:

> *We shall not cease from exploration*
> *And the end of all our exploration*
> *Will be to arrive where we started*
> *And know the place for the first time.*

### Fear

When we venture outside our comfort zone we enter the unknown. The unknown usually provokes fear. That's normal. But fear is a place we must walk through to become whole. It is just another address in our minds, one more place in the vast city of consciousness. There are many other places in that city that are not at all fearful. But first we must get by the fear. It's always the first house on the street. Much of the fear we feel is in the anticipation of an event rather than in the experience itself. If we let fear stop us we will fail in our ultimate purpose. We will fail to grow.

## The Healing Process

When I work with clients I always begin by having them lay down on my healing table. I place one hand under the base of their spine, the other under the base of their skull. As soon as my hands make contact with their body the healing power starts flowing through me into them. Within a few minutes they usually become very relaxed. In most cases they will feel a sense of warmth, or heat, gently flowing through their body as the healing energy is directed into them. Sometimes they also feel a sense of tingling or electricity flowing through them.

As the healing energy flows into them it fills them with light. The light in their bodies allows me to see clairvoyantly where the energy blocks are buried in their system. These blocks hold and conceal past trauma. When I see these blocks I often see pictures in my mind's eye that show me what happened to cause these blocks to form.

Recently a semi-retired chiropractic physician came in

to see me. He had been praying for a long time to find the right person to help him heal his life. Then one day he turned on the TV in Los Angeles where he lived and saw me being interviewed. His intuition told him he had found the right person when he heard me speak.

When he came in he was suffering from hydro-nephritis of the kidneys and prostate cancer which had spread to his bones. He was in a great deal of pain at the time. His doctors had told him he had from one to three years of life left and would have to take a lot of drugs and radiation to last that long. Needless to say he wasn't exactly joyous after hearing their prognosis.

In the beginning of our work together he had little energy and constant, chronic pain. His face was pinched and pained and lined with stress. His eyes were dim and cloudy. He was generally depressed and had little hope.

As we started working the energy flowing into him would bring up all the dark, buried areas of his psyche. As that darkness surfaced his pain would intensify. Old memories long silent and repressed, flooded into his consciousness. It was as if a huge dam had broken in his psyche. He found himself reliving forgotten aspects of his childhood. Both his parents were alcoholics, angry and abusive. His father beat him. His mother blamed all her problems on the fact that he was born. He never had a chance. Reliving these memories brought up rivers of suppressed grief. Sometimes he'd sob. Sometimes he'd scream. Sometimes the pain would race from spot to spot throughout his body. As the sessions progressed it seemed that he was getting worse not better.

When he felt that way I would always remind him of the first principle of transformational healing. When the light enters your body it brings up your pain. Nothing within can hide from the power of that light. The fact that he felt worse actually meant he was getting better. As the pain travels up to the surface from the places where it has been buried one becomes more conscious of it and feels it more intensely. We have to reconnect with it and feel it consciously to discharge and overcome it. He felt worse but I knew he was getting better. The old trauma that had secretly dominated his life was being processed and discharged from his system.

Finally after several sessions the pain began to diminish. He started feeling better and had more energy. I also noticed something happening that was more subtle, but very important for his growth. When he had first come to me I had observed that he had a wall up around his heart. He wasn't about to let anyone get close to him. He was scared of loving and being loved. But now that he had finally faced his parent's rejection and acts of hatred toward him he had been able to release the trauma and toxic nature of his childhood. As he was able to let go at last of what his parents had done to him his heart opened and flowered.

As the healing process continued he became more alive. The stress went out of his face, wrinkles disappeared and his color went from ashen gray to rosy pink. His eyes became very bright blue where they once had been dull gray embers. All of a sudden people wanted to be around him, talk to him and hug him. When I heard him tell his stories about how other people were now reacting to him I just smiled. "Bill," I said. (Not his real name.) "You have become at last what you were always meant to be. A Beacon of Love." When we heal we become a channel for unconditional love and become in our turn a healer.

And finally we received the best news of all. He went back to see his doctors and was retested for the cancer that had been ravaging his system. His PSA, the standard test for prostate antibodies that often indicates the presence of prostate cancer if it is over a reading of four, came back at .67, the reading of a teenager in perfect health. A Cat scan and MRI showed no sign of cancer in his bones. None whatsoever. He had his health back. Shortly after those results came back Bill told me that his spine, which had been crooked and curved all his life had almost completely straightened out. There was just one small place in his upper thoracic vertebrae that hadn't yet straightened out.

In healing his life Bill also transformed his consciousness. The hidden trauma buried in the unconscious areas of his psyche no longer held him back in either his march toward fulfillment or in his quest for health. The negative weight that had anchored his life in pain and misery from the time of his childhood had been overcome. As he shed that psychic weight he made up for lost time rising high on the scale of the vertical ascent in a short period of time.

## The Beacon Program

When I work with clients it is usually for a minimum of ten sessions. Ten sessions give me a chance to get some real work done and help my clients make lasting progress. However, clients are not limited to ten sessions. They can have as many as they feel they need. But ten is the base number. I call this program of transformational healing The Beacon Program.

Around the same time that Bill found me on TV another client, a woman in her mid thirties, discovered me in a similar manner. She was home one afternoon when a strong feeling came over her to turn on Channel 3 on her TV. She thought that very strange, as she wasn't used to being prompted from within to do such things. Her doubt notwithstanding, she turned on the tube and there I was. She called after the show.

At the time of our initial contact she was desperate, depressed and suicidal. She told me during that first phone conversation that she was scheduled to start a conventional psychotherapy program the next day. However, she had been through enough standard therapy before and really didn't want to do it again. It hadn't really helped her very much. She asked if I would take her on. We started our work together later that week.

As our sessions progressed and the healing energy poured into her much of her buried traumatic material rose to the surface as it had with Bill. Her father had been cold, distant and highly critical of her. He had wanted a son. He got a daughter. In his eyes she couldn't do anything right. No matter what she did to get his love he continued to disapprove of her. Her mother was somewhat emotionally detached from her. There wasn't much warmth in her home.

When she was a little girl a woman friend of her mother's sexually abused her. She didn't receive much nurturing as a child. She was lonely and on her own emotionally.

As the sessions continued this material flooded into her consciousness. She found herself even more depressed than before. One day she walked in and said, "I don't think this is working for me. I seem to be getting worse. Maybe I should stop."

"The fact that it's seeming to get worse is simply a sign that you are getting much better," I replied. "I know that sounds contradictory but this is how the transformation process works. If you want to be happy, you must find the places within you that are sad and unhappy. If you want to be whole, you must seek out those places where you are fragmented. If you want to be free you must go to those places inside your unconscious where you are bound. In the transformation process you find what you want by owning what you don't want. When you enter the Transformation Zone you move toward the negative side of your psyche. If you don't engage your negativity you will never be the master in your own house. The Beacon Program takes you into the Transformation Zone (T Zone) and helps you find your freedom. The fact that your pain has increased means that it has come fully to the surface and is being discharged. You can't release what you can't feel. But if you stop now that material will continue to cling to your psyche and hold you down in these dark, depressed emotional states. I don't think that's what you want. Soon enough it will be all gone. Have faith."

She did. Two sessions later she came to my office a different person. She was glowing and filled with light and happiness. "If I hadn't experienced this work I never would have believed it. You were right. I feel wonderful. It was worth what I had to go through, many times over."

It always is. On the other side of pain and suffering there is a new future and a new life that is always better than the life you have outgrown.

At our ninth session she reported that she no longer had the asthma that had bothered her almost all her life. "My friends notice the change in me too. Many of them have remarked that I look radiant and seem much more powerful. It used to be that whenever I looked inside myself I would see these doors that I would be terrified of opening.

If I opened one of them I would find myself lost in darkness and it could take months before I could get out of deep depression. Now I look inside and I'm not at all afraid. I can open any door and all I find is light. I feel great."

Then I said something to her that I'm sure she found somewhat strange. "Look at your feet,"I said. "Do you notice how your high your arch is and how your toes pull back toward your legs?"

"Yes," she replied. "They've always been like that. So what?"

"Over the years I've seen feet like that on many people. It usually indicates you have had a lifetime in China where your feet were bound. Would like me to unbind them?"

"You can do that?"

"Sure. I'll just put my hands on your feet and the healing power will straighten them out."

"Just like that?"

"Why not?"

"Well, everything else you said came true. I guess there's nothing to lose. Let's give it a shot."

I put my hands on each foot, one at a time, and let the

healing power flow into her feet. It only took a few minutes per foot. "OK. We're done with that. It'll take a few days for the energy blocks in your feet to dissipate and the muscles and bones in your feet to realign themselves. Let's see what happens."

When she came in for her final session she was glowing. Her eyes were very bright and her cheeks very rosy. "If I hadn't seen what happened for myself I would never have believed you. Look at my feet," She said, as she took off her shoes and got on the table. Her feet were now normal and her toes were no longer pointing backwards toward her legs. In that final session she didn't cry or feel any pain. Instead she found herself floating in a bright white light feeling free and at peace.

## The T Zone

The T Zone is not about enjoying yourself. It turns you upside down and shakes you free of what you no longer need to carry. It is a zone you must walk through to rectify your life, make yourself whole and master the vertical scale. The T Zone experience is crucial to evolution and personal fulfillment.

The Beacon Program is a powerful method for crossing that zone safely and quickly.

# CHAPTER FOUR

## The Vertical Ascent

The base of the vertical scale is a depressed emotional environment, filled with negativity, powerlessness and hopelessness. No one wants to live in that bleak neighborhood but many people find themselves trapped there nevertheless. Unfortunately, it's not an easy place to leave. Those who spend their lives in this dark psychological space are trapped in an internal feedback system of great complexity that appears to seal off all possible escape routes.

The residents of this self-imposed purgatory are convinced they can't change the way things are. Life seems hopeless, even doomed. Dark veils obscure their internal perception. It is as if they were living in a basement with no windows to let in the light and no door to let them out. In an environment like this there is no room for truth, hope or love to grow. Without any inner light to see the way out of this psychological conundrum it is difficult to change the way things seem to be.

### How We Create a Personal Reality System

A client of mine, named Ruth, suffered repeated sexual abuse at the hands of her father when she was a child. This led her to create an unconscious, personal reality system based on three linked primary beliefs. The first belief cautioned that the world is a very unsafe place. The second belief warned that people are not to be trusted. The third belief screamed, "be especially wary of those who say they love you. They are the ones who will hurt you the most."

The buried emotional content in Ruth's unconscious that generated these three beliefs was highly charged. Thirty years later this content retains its intensity. Time has not diminished its effect on Ruth's life. What has changed is that Ruth is no longer in touch with the causative experience and the trauma created in her psyche because of it. Through a mysterious autonomous psychic process those emotions have been removed from her conscious mind and placed in the unconscious side of her psyche where they remain active and influential. The autonomous movement of emotional material from the conscious side of the psyche to the unconscious side creates the gaps in our being. These gaps split the psyche so that its conscious and unconscious aspects are no longer working together toward the same goal of success and fulfillment but at cross purposes to each other.

### Covert Action in the Unconscious

When emotional content is transferred from the conscious to the unconscious it becomes more virulent than ever because it is now *freed* of all restraints and can operate in a *covert* manner. With no preventative mechanism or monitoring system existent in the unconscious to harness or contain the destructive power of this buried emotional content it is able to create more painful events in our life.

Ruth consciously wants to be happy and involved and can't understand why it seems so impossible for her to get what she wants. She doesn't realize that her unconscious mind has a competing agenda. It wants her to feel safe and be free of terror. To reach that goal it prompts her to avoid life, distance herself from those who love her and turn away from commitment to a career. She is caught between two competing visions. Whenever the psyche is divided between a conscious goal and an unconscious agenda it is the unconscious agenda that controls the balance of power. *The negative will prevail in our life until the psyche is healed and brought back to balance.* If we do not choose to heal the trauma stored in the unconscious side of the psyche we will be the victim of that trauma over and over again.

### The Equation of Healing

Healing moves in the opposite direction from that of the wounding process, shifting emotional content from the dark unconscious side of the psyche back to the conscious side. In healing the psyche of its internal splits and gaps we must take back our power from the forces that originally fragmented it. If we don't take back our power it may leak out of the psyche and be used against us. "Power leaks" push us further down the vertical scale rather than assisting us to ascend it.

### Power Leaks and Addictive Behavior

The greatest weapon at our disposal against pain and suffering is not drugs or denial but consciousness. Addictions, such as drug use or alcohol abuse, are evidence of a lack of consciousness and often indicate a "power leak" in the psyche of devastating consequences. Addictions are the flawed attempt to stop the pain of being psychologically fragmented. If the addict had succeeded in taking back his power he wouldn't have the need or the temptation to engage in addictive behavior. Remember, *it takes all our power to become more conscious.* When power leaks out of the psyche the individual so effected will tend to feel alone, desperate, incapable of handling his life and in need of a fix. Power leaks are caused by unhealed trauma deposited in

the unconscious side of the psyche that we have not faced
• and overcome. The more we let our power leak into addictive behavior the more tenuous becomes the tie between
the past, where the cause of our addictive behavior lies, and
the present, where addictive behavior patterns may be
destroying our lives.

## The Crucial Link Between Past and Present

As time passes the internal link between current problems and past events becomes more difficult to resurrect.
During the passage of time layers of psychic sediment are
deposited over traumatic emotional experiences. These layers sever the tie between conscious awareness and past
events. Without re-establishing that connection it is very
difficult to shift the balance of power from the unconscious
back to the conscious side of the psyche. No matter what
beneficial changes may have occurred in our external situation the power of the unresolved past to extend its tendrils
into the present and exert its destructive influence at any
moment is always present.

Ruth's experience of childhood abuse has controlled
and dictated her adult experience. Because of this problem
her adulthood has been as negative as her childhood was
painful. The three beliefs that were formed in her childhood still control her unconscious personal reality system,
keeping her isolated from other people, depressed and
unhappy. She is addicted to eating. Eating dulls her feelings. When she eats chocolate she feels better.

## Attachment and Unconsciousness

Ruth is still involved in her childhood experience *even if she doesn't know it.* Carl Jung once wrote, in his Commentary on The Secret Of The Golden Flower, "Wherever we are still attached, we are still possessed; and when we are possessed, there is one stronger than us who possesses us." Ruth is indeed possessed by the unconscious contents of her psyche. Time does not diminish the power of what is buried in the unconscious. If anything time empowers and strengthens the contents of the unconscious. A power leak that at the time seems miniscule, like a trickle of water coming through a dam, over time becomes a torrent that is much more difficult to repair.

## Psychic Splits and Life Strategies

When Ruth split off the childhood experiences of sexual abuse from her conscious mind and buried them in her unconscious, she lost her power to be whole. The split caused by her experience of being sexually abused created a significant gap in her consciousness that she could not cross and could not heal. This rupture lead to an important transfer of power within her psyche. It caused the creative power in her life to shift from what she consciously wanted to achieve (become a doctor like her father) to what the *fear* embedded in her unconscious wanted to prevent from ever happening to her again. As a result, her life strategy downshifted from how to succeed and fulfill herself, to how to survive and endure her life. Instead of being proactive and positive she became defensive and reactive. Rather than going for what she wanted, she went into hiding so she couldn't be hurt. The irony is that she has never stopped hurting. She has chosen a life of terror over a life of power. Instead of making a contribution to the world that would enhance her self-esteem she sits alone in her house eating chocolates to mask her shame and medicate the pain of having no self-esteem. Ruth has a serious power leak. Her problem will not go away. It will just get larger.

## Unconscious Decisions

All these important life decisions occurred on the unconscious level of Ruth's psyche. The power of the positive was replaced by the power of the negative because the equilibrium of her psyche had been subverted by the abuse she suffered in childhood. The negative had gained the upper hand. Ruth's experience illuminates the covert, creative functions of the unconscious side of the human psyche. While the content of our personal experience is unique the laws of the psyche are not. They apply to each of us, without exception.

Everyone experiences some form of trauma in his or her life. If we factor in the likelihood that we have had other lifetimes in which we experienced painful events that were not resolved, then the very real possibility exists that there are several sites in the unconscious where old, forgotten trauma has been deposited. This trauma would include material from this life as well as events from previous lives.

## Karma and Death

Our Karma consists of the internal chains that bind us. Karma does not end with death. The physical body dies but consciousness survives. Death changes little about our state of consciousness (or lack of consciousness), except its location, which shifts from the physical plane to a non-physical destination. During this shift of location the landscape of the unconscious remains firmly intact. The great mystic poet Kabir, writing in the fourteenth century put it this way:

> *What you call "salvation" belongs to the time*
> *before death.*
>
> *If you don't break your ropes while you're alive,*
> *do you think ghosts*
> *will do it after?*
>
> *The idea that the soul will join with the ecstatic*
> *just because the body is rotten – that is all fantasy.*
>
> *What is found now is found then.*
>
> *If you find nothing now, you will simply end up with*
> *an apartment in the city of death.*

When we are reborn in another time and in another body the same unconscious content or karma returns with our soul. This content will control our lives until we transform it. Death does not end this tyranny. It only interrupts it. In dealing with karma we should keep the following dictum in mind, "A chain is only as strong as its weakest link." The weakest link is always that which we have buried in our bodies and refused to deal with.

Our refusal to heal our consciousness creates a future that always mirrors our internal pain and fragmentation. If we let our power leak out we will not have the power we need to move forward. An absence of power leads to a preponderance of pain. When we are powerless we are vulnerable to addictive behavior. We can never truly escape ourselves but we can choose, at any moment, to face ourselves. The sooner we choose to do so the easier it will be to close the gaps in our psyche.

## The Victim Syndrome

For Ruth the weak link of being abused as a child will continue to control her life until she chooses to stop casting herself in the role of the unconscious victim. This may not seem like fair play. After all, she was an innocent victim. She didn't ask to be abused. Why should she be the one to suffer? Why, indeed? These are legitimate questions, but very dangerous from the healing perspective. Asking why over and over again in the form of *why* did it happen, or *why* me, only increases the torment and adds to the sense of powerlessness. If we fall into this self-indulgent trap we may never find the way out. The continual hand wringing suggested by *the lament of why* is a preoccupation we can ill afford. It is the cry of the victim drowning in self-pity.

### The Right Question

We come to the right question when we stop asking why and make a simple, straightforward statement about our predicament. "Something horrible happened to me. *What* can I do about it?" This statement is a simple declaration of acceptance. It marks a crucial step in the healing process because the ability to accept the reality of a situation is the beginning of the power to change that reality. Acceptance is the basis of effective action. If we're asking why, we are still enmeshed in the situation and have not yet accepted what happened.

The "why" state is one of helplessness and ineffectiveness. Asking what can I do to heal myself is positive. It's a question that lays the basis for taking back our power, rather than continuing to give it away. In Ruth's case, confronting the pain buried in her unconscious may not be desirable, but it is necessary. It is her way out, the positive thing she can do to free herself. Remember, lest you feel sorry for her, or for yourself if you are in a similar situation, that at least there is a way out.

Life is not really hopeless. It only appears that way when we are at the bottom of the vertical scale. If Ruth is to get her life back on course she must restore the power usurped by the unconscious side of her psyche. If she refuses to feel her pain there can be no transformation. Healing depends on feeling.

## Transformation and the Ability to Feel

Transformational healing is an emotional process. Emotions are *not* healed by the conscious mind. Whenever we evaluate or describe our feelings from the point of view of the conscious mind we are maintaining a discreet distance from those feelings. At those times we are not feeling our emotions but filtering them through the rational brain. Description is observation, in itself a form of distancing in which we create a separation between subject and object so we may better evaluate and quantify what we study. While it might be the scientific method it is certainly not the type of emotional encounter that transformation requires. Transformational healing requires emotional involvement, not scientific aloofness. In the transformational process there can be no distancing from our feelings. Emotional aloofness keeps the negative emotional content stored in the unconscious active and alive in our lives. Being verbal, articulate and rational about our feelings is a step forward, nothing more. It may give us a degree of insight into our problems. It is not the solution.

To heal ourselves we must close the distance in our psyche between where we have stored those feelings and where we feel them. This means that we must shift our focus from the rational mind where we are safely in control to the unconscious areas of the psyche where we have no control.

## Sound and Power

One method to accomplish this task is to have the client make nonverbal sounds while the healer focuses the healing energy on the areas of the body where the buried material has been stored. These sounds open the doors of the psyche so that the buried rage, fear and terror entombed in the body can speak in its own language. By allowing this negative content to speak in its own tongue, unedited and uncensored by the rational mind, it can be exorcised from the psyche.

The healing energy brings the hidden blocks that contain these emotions to the surface and softens them, allowing their emotional content to spill out. As the toxic energy is discharged the healing power sweeps it out of the client's system and replaces it with energy of very high quality and purity. The new energy closes the gap in the client's psyche allowing him to take another step forward on the vertical scale of conscious evolution. The combination of sound and healing energy is extremely powerful. When the negative contents of the psyche are allowed to have their day in the sun, they diminish and die.

There is little forward movement in the healing process until the dark side of the psyche is engaged. To go forward, we must go back. To reach the light we must overcome the darkness. To be whole we must find the places where we are wounded. We *increase* the positive side of consciousness by confronting the negative content of the unconscious. Our body is either a tomb of darkness or a vessel of light. It is our choice to make.

Some years ago I went to Kansas City to lead a healing workshop. Among those participating in the workshop was a woman in her mid fifties who had been operated on recently for a cancerous tumor on her thyroid. The tumor had been successfully removed but she looked dreadful. Her face was ashen gray, her eyes sunken and lifeless. It was obvious she wasn't well.

When her time came to get on the healing table I had the three other members of her team put their hands on specific areas of her torso and head where I could see several areas of blocked energy. As the healing energy flowed into these areas the contents of her unconscious were gradually mobilized and started to emerge. At this point something unusual occurred in her unconscious. She assumed another identity to deal with the emotional content that was coming up. While this switch in identity was a peculiar development it is not entirely without precedent.

The unconscious contains a multitude of identities. Sometimes a client will process events from other lifetimes by unconsciously assuming a former identity from that lifetime as he discharges the trauma. This releases the identity as well as the trauma that occurred while the soul was in that identity. In other cases, if the trauma buried in the unconscious created deep and persistent feelings of shame and inferiority, clients will sometimes respond by adopting an identity that enables them to feel superior in that situation. The feeling of superiority permits them to feel less threatened as they release their pain. The adoption of an identity is invariably an unconscious decision that happens automatically.

With the healing energy mobilizing her unconscious trauma this woman took on the identity of St. Francis and began blessing her mother who had treated her badly as a child. She also blessed many other people in her life that had harmed her, made the sign of the cross several times and went into prayer.

She told me later, after her session was over, that she had grown up in Europe. Her mother had been a very religious Catholic who prayed to St. Francis daily. Now the fact that her unconscious had chosen the identity of St. Francis began to make sense. St. Francis had been the power in her mother's life. What better way to work out her power and inferiority issues with her mother than to assume the identity of the person her mother had given her power to? If she was St. Francis she was now the power in her mother's life. This transfer of identity allowed her to process the contents of her unconscious from a position of strength.

When she assumed the identity of St. Francis the other members in her group were thrown off balance by her strange behavior and had no idea how to respond to her. I told them to keep on doing what they were doing. Her actions confirmed that healing events were taking place in her psyche and should not be interrupted. She was moving through an unconscious site where trauma had been buried, nothing more. I told them to go along with her and be patient. When she was done processing the material deposited at that site she would come back to herself.

About twenty minutes later she closed her eyes and lay down flat on the table, not moving a muscle, no longer speaking. Her business at that unconscious site was finished. When she returned to normal consciousness a little later she was very peaceful and happy. I saw her the next day at a meeting of the fellowship that had sponsored my visit. She did not look like the same person she had been the day before. The gray pallor was gone. So were the hollow, burned out eyes. Her color was normal, her cheeks rosy, and her eyes bright. She was animated, alive, filled with energy and obviously happy. She had confronted a difficult place in her unconscious and was reaping the reward.

### The Need to Choose

Ruth's case, unfortunately, is different. She hasn't fully engaged her unconscious trauma yet and entered the T Zone. She is not destined to a life of pain and futility unless her fear paralyzes her will to change. Life circumstances can always change. That's the beauty of a Duality System. Despite what may have happened in the past we can always choose to change and transfer our power back from the unconscious to the conscious mind. When we do we can move forward again. Nothing is fixed in life and nothing is forever.

There is no virtue in staying a victim, no matter what may have happened. If we don't take responsibility for ourselves nothing will change. The victim lives at the bottom of the vertical scale. If he accepts what happened to him and takes responsibility for healing his problem he is on the path that leads out of the darkness. If he chooses to blame others, he is writing himself a prescription for constant, chronic pain.

# CHAPTER FIVE

## Reality and the Power of Beliefs

What we have internalized as true in the personal reality system of the unconscious may not be necessarily true in the objective, external world. Whether or not it is true in the external world is not of great importance with regard to the creative dynamic of the psyche. What is important in this psychic scheme is that it is true in our internal world because the source of personal reality is the externalization of unconscious, subjective beliefs. Whether we recognize it or not, we are the creative power in our life. Whatever is true in our unconscious is true in our lives. We are never victims, unless we *choose* to be.

## A Crucial Feedback System

The unbreakable connection between unconscious belief and personal reality constitutes a powerful feedback system in which what we experience is the feedback of what we believe. We are the prisoners of our negative beliefs. If we fail to grasp either the reality or the mechanics of this feedback system it is easy to say when the next bad thing happens in our life, "See! No matter how hard I work nothing works out. I just can't get ahead. No one likes me." Fortified by this confirmation in the world of "objective" experience it is easy to see ourselves as victims of life when the reality is that we have created a life of victimization. Internalized truth is often dangerous because it is not our real truth. Our real inner truth only emerges when we have healed and overcome the traumatic material buried in the personal reality system of the unconscious. When we have successfully taken back our power and integrated the psyche our inner truth finally surfaces.

## The Downward Spiral

The negative experiences created from the negative beliefs formulated in the personal reality system strengthen the negative beliefs we hold about ourselves. A belief in failure is reinforced and strengthened by each new confirming negative experience. As this process continues we lose more of our personal power as our reality continually confirms our internalized truth.

## Responsibility and Change

If we refuse to see our role in creating our experience we will be unable to take responsibility for improving our life. As I have stressed throughout this book, without taking personal responsibility nothing changes for the better. Things will only get worse. We will stay in the basement of the vertical scale, feeling victimized and sorry for ourselves, programmed for more failure.

Whatever we do, *life will continue to support our version of truth*. This is a profound truth. **Life always supports us**. But there is a catch. That support is dependent on our personal truth. The nature of the personal truth in our unconscious determines the quality and level of the support that life will give us. If the nature of our personal truth is negative the support life gives us will also be negative. On the other hand, if the nature of our personal truth is positive the support life gives us will also be positive.

## The Nature of Personal Truth

Since everyone's experience is unique the personal truth we live is also unique. If all personal truth has unique dimensions then our personal truth is relative, not absolute. If we change our beliefs our personal truth will also change. This means the truth is relative in at least two ways. First everyone's truth is somewhat different and unique. Second we can change our unconscious beliefs and experience a new, higher truth in our lives. Personal *truth is relative and flexible. It allows for change and growth.* Remember that we live in a Duality System ruled by change and uncertainty. The purpose of life is growth. As we grow our truth grows with us. It gets lighter, brighter, and wider as we move up the vertical scale.

At the top of the vertical truth there is virtually no difference between personal and universal truth. That is because as we grow we grow from the personal toward the universal. We escape our personal selves by finding our truth. And what we find at the summit of the vertical scale is that we are one with the Oneness of Life. The Oneness includes us and everything else that exists. There is no separation at all. It only *appears* that way while our psyche is fragmented and gaps remain in our consciousness. This is the illusion we all must deal with on the physical plane. Since the truth is not apparent on the physical plane growth towards the Oneness is a challenge. Because there is no separation in universal reality there is no room for judgment. There is only room for unconditional love. On the higher planes of consciousness everything thrives because all that exists there exists in divine order. It is not so here.

### Overcoming the Tyranny of the Past

Frank was in bad shape when he first came in to see me.

His second marriage had just broken up and he had lost virtually everything he had worked his whole life for. While he was out to sea his wife had emptied his bank accounts, taken his rare coin collection, jewelry, car and left. He was in his mid-fifties and had been in the merchant marine since he was eighteen.

When we began our work together the first layer of emotional material that came up concerned his childhood rather than his marriage. Both parents, like Bill's, were alcoholics. His father was angry, distant and verbally demeaning. His mother was also angry and abusive. She would say things to him like, "You're so ugly no woman would ever want you. You'll never be able to keep a woman," and "You'll never amount to anything in life." There was nothing warm and safe about his childhood. Often there was no food for breakfast and he'd go to school hungry.

As these memories surfaced he was able to feel the hidden grief, hurt and rage attached to his childhood. While he lay on the table with the healing energy pouring into him and the buried pain pouring out of him he would turn every which way as the twisted parts of his childhood slowly untwisted and straightened themselves out.

While he was turning his psyche around and healing the gaps in his being an exciting new pattern began to emerge in his life. He received several promotions at work. In more than thirty previous years at sea he had never risen higher than third mate. Now in rapid order he went from third mate, to second mate, to first mate, to master and captain. His income doubled. The tyrannical voice of his mother screaming silently in his unconscious for more than five decades, "You'll never amount to anything in life!" was finally muted and put to rest.

As he won the war for control of his inner world he gained more control in his outer life. He didn't have to fight for that control or climb the ladder to success in the ordinary way. He did not seek any of his promotions. They came to him, naturally and unexpectedly, as if they were part of the natural order of things. His reality shifted upward to conform to his new belief system. His self image also shifted upward from the negative image he had internalized from his parents to a newer positive sense of self. He no longer was a victim of subjective, internalized truth. Instead he was in touch with his inner truth. As he shifted from being lead by his internalized truth to following his inner truth his life became positive and more fulfilling.

Frank's profound shift was not an accident. It occurred because he took responsibility for what had happened in his childhood. He stopped hating and blaming his parents. He exercised his responsibility by confronting the reality system hidden in his unconscious. He had absorbed the higher healing light I had transferred into him, used it to discharge the heavy unresolved energies afflicting him, and closed important gaps in his consciousness. By closing these gaps he was able to take back his power from the unconscious side of the psyche. He was no longer dominated by what he didn't want but opened to the possibility of what he did want.

One of the important things Frank learned during his experience in the T Zone was that he hadn't walked away from his childhood and his parents when he went out to sea as he had thought. He had just buried his trauma in his body where it continued to wreak havoc in his life. He also saw that as a child he had built a crust around himself so no one would be able to get inside his defenses and hurt him again. All this, of course, had happened unconsciously. The ramifications in his life, however, had been enormous. All his adult life he had been depressed and terrified of people, afraid that they would find out how awful and terrible he was then abandon him. His fear of rejection had lead him to choose to go through life a loner.

After we completed a certain stage in his healing I suggested that he come to the monthly healing workshops which many of my clients attended. Before long Frank became a mainstay at these workshops. When he went out to sea and couldn't attend the workshops many of the women would ask where he was. The real Frank was a kind, grounded, decent man. Everyone felt safe with him. He also brought out the mothering instinct in many of the women because they all wanted to hug and nurture him.

No woman ever felt that way about him before he went through the T Zone. The women he formerly had attracted were only those who fulfilled his mother's vicious prophecy, "You're so ugly no woman will ever want you." Now only good, loving women were attracted to him. It was effortless on his part. He wasn't even trying. Eventually, he was asked by his union to go to Washington to lobby the federal government to help save the merchant marine. He would have to talk to senators and congressmen if he agreed to go. Before his healing he would have found the experience highly intimidating. Now he took a deep breath, went and did it, and did it well.

Through his healing Frank had discovered one of the great secrets of the vertical scale. When you confront and overcome the dark unconscious side of the psyche that ails and assails you, you not only find fulfillment but greater success.

Frank was fortunate. He had the wisdom to confront his unconscious and me to help him through the T Zone. When we're children we bury awful things in our body so we can survive, endure and go on. Often, a survival strategy is our only option. But if that's all we ever do our future will not be any better than our past. No matter what we may achieve the gaps in our psyche will remain intact and the same deep-rooted feelings of childhood shame and powerlessness will continue to be the power in our lives. To the extent that we root our life strategy in the perspective that it's best to endure and survive, rather than remember and feel, the past is kept alive. Leaving home and going out to sea didn't end Frank's problems. Instead they dominated his life for more than fifty years.

## The Difficult Bind

We are all bound by the internalized truth embedded in the personal reality system of the unconscious. The secret to changing our lives is to change the schematics of the unconscious. We must close the gaps in our being. Many people think that affirmations and visualizations will accomplish the necessary changes in the unconscious. Unfortunately, these techniques change little in the unconscious. But the little they change allows people to delude themselves into thinking that everything has been corrected.

Jane came to me on the recommendation of her therapist. When I put my hands on her spine at the beginning of her first session I could see a big knot of energy in her pelvic region. I intuitively knew the block had to do with unfinished business with her mother. I could see that her mother had been verbally cruel to her as a young child consistently negating her and destroying her self-esteem. I shifted my hands to her pelvic region, placing one hand on the base of her spine, the other a few inches below her navel. I said to her, "What can you tell me about your mother?"

"She was a big problem for me," she replied. "But I took care of that in therapy."

"That's good," I said. "There's some blocked energy in your pelvis. Put your attention on that area and tell me how it feels."

She was quiet for a moment before answering. "It feels sort of thick and congested. There's a vague sense of uneasiness there too."

"OK" I said. "From where you're feeling the uneasiness, make a soft sort of moaning sound. Just keep the sound going and let yourself go where it takes you. Whatever your body wants to do let it do. Do not censor your movements or sounds in any way. Just go with what comes out of your body."

She started to moan softly. Within a few minutes her consciousness shifted into an entirely different space. She curled into a fetal position, lying on her side, with her feet curled up to her chest and started crying and screaming at her mother. As she went into this major gap in her psyche the healing energy flowing through me became very hot and intense, appearing like a bright red spiritual fire. The energy was burning up the negativity buried in her pelvis. She sweated profusely. After a time, perhaps forty minutes, she came back to her normal level of consciousness and lay flat on the table. The energy flowing through me shifted to accommodate the change in her consciousness. I could see a blue and white energy pouring through me. Jane became very calm and peaceful as the blue and white light flowed through her. When we finished some moments later her eyes became very bright. The stress and sense of unease was gone from her face. She looked altogether different.

"How do you feel?" I asked.

"I'm not sure." She responded. "I've never felt this way. I feel so light. I'm physically exhausted, but I've got all sorts of energy. My body feels very warm. I'm tingling all over."

"I think that stuff with your mother is out of your system now."

"Yeah, that was amazing!" she said. "I had no idea that was in me. I thought I had healed it years ago."

### The Power of the Higher Healing Light

That's the point. Until the higher healing light of the spirit brings the repressed material of the unconscious to the surface of the conscious mind we often have no idea that it's deep inside us silently working its dark magic in our lives. Even if we've been in therapy there's no guarantee that the blocks in our body have been discharged or that their negative influence in our lives has been overcome.

Sometimes therapy wraps us in the comforting yet dangerous illusion that we've overcome our inner demons when the reality is we've just touched their surface. As in Jane's case, deeper levels of unresolved psychic material often lie hidden inside us where the conventional tools of therapy cannot always reach. The advantage of working with the higher healing light is threefold. First, it brings up whatever is hidden in the unconscious. Nothing can hide from the Higher Light of Spirit. Second, it discharges negative, unresolved energy from our system. Third, it replaces that negative energy with positive power from a source higher than we are normally capable of contacting. The new positive energy integrates and unifies the psyche, thrusting us higher up the vertical scale. The result is that both our present life and our entire evolution is upgraded.

## The Evolutionary Leap

The result of walking through the T Zone is an evolutionary leap in consciousness. We enter the T Zone when we make conscious contact with the negative side of our nature. The T Zone is the place of inner confrontation, where we can finally heal ourselves, and significantly improve the quality of our life experience.

## The Bridge Across the Psyche

The main purpose of life on this planet is to reconstruct the missing link in our psyche and claim our connection to the Oneness. The only way we can complete this mission is to build the inner bridge across the psyche to the Spirit. To accomplish this critical life task we have chosen to subject ourselves to the peculiar constraints of the Duality System that regulates life on this planet. The uncertainty that is a dominant feature of the Duality System is also a powerful goad to growth.

An oyster creates a pearl because the sand in its shell makes it uncomfortable. We choose to heal our consciousness because in the final analysis life without a connection to the Oneness is not only uncomfortable but also unsustainable. The inner bridge to that Oneness is built by overcoming the dark congested emotional energies that have created the ruptures and splits in our psyche in the first place. If we neglect the essential task of building the inner bridge we will fail in the spiritual purpose of life. That is why Christ, in his wisdom said, "Seek Ye first the Kingdom of Heaven and all else will be added unto you." And then later, also asked, "What good does it do a man to gain the whole world and lose his soul?"

### The Right Dreams

If we don't dream the right dreams we will never find the way that leads from the darkness to the light. We pay a very high price to remain unconscious and disconnected from our destiny. The tragedy is that we are unaware of the price of our unconsciousness. God is everywhere, but we ignore Him. We are too busy being split and fragmented. God seeks to help and empower us, but we do not seek Him. We are too busy with the business of getting ahead, plotting our future, and fighting with each other for what we want. We are not living life in the fast lane as we think we are. We are living life in the lost lane. What is it we have created in this world if not bedlam? And who has made it that way if not us?

# CHAPTER SIX

## The Ego

The ego is very aware of its fragile grip over our lives and knows it needs to keep us disconnected from the Oneness to survive. Its degree of security is in direct proportion to the degree of our internal fragmentation. It therefore has a vested interest in keeping us fragmented and split. Its continued existence depends on it.

Interestingly enough, the ego is itself a creation of the psyche. Its original purpose was to manage our inner separation from spirit. To accomplish this task it was given a dual mandate. First, it was charged with protecting us from external events that might frighten us or jeopardize our survival. Second, it was given the responsibility for keeping our internal trauma securely encased in the landscape of the body so we wouldn't have to feel it or deal with it again. An important aspect of this second level of responsibility was its role in keeping the unconscious personal reality system intact and operable.

Both areas of the ego's mandate concern fear management. Internally the ego must keep our fear down, where we can't feel it. Externally it must keep fear out, so we won't feel it. This puts the ego in a catch 22 situation. Unconscious trauma is highly charged and attracts more negativity to us. Thus, what the ego is commissioned to avoid (more negative situations) it automatically creates.

This is good for the ego, because it increases the internal fragmentation of the psyche, and bad for us, because it makes reconnection with the Oneness seem impossible. Of course, the ego would like nothing better than for us to believe that the possibility of reconnection does not exist because the Oneness itself does not exist. "God is Dead. There is no God," are both statements of an ego presiding over a fractured psyche.

It is obvious that the ego cannot succeed in its assigned task. It can't manage fear, but it can duplicate and multiply those fears in an endless parade of experiences and life events. Ironically, it is the ego's failure to protect us that insures its success. As the fragmentation process in the psyche continues it creates more internal insecurity. One needs to turn somewhere. "Over here!" screams the ego confidently. Relieved that someone in the psyche seems to know what he is doing, we permit the ego to assume more control. As we lose our intrinsic power the ego becomes more powerful.

## Ego and the Loss of Emotion

In performing its mission of managing fear the ego deprives us of our capacity to utilize the full spectrum of feeling because it keeps much or our emotional energy bound up in buried trauma. There are serious consequences to the restriction and repression of our feeling nature. First, the early warning system of the intuition, which depends on our awareness of subtle levels of feeling as its prime means of communication, is thoroughly incapacitated. Because of the ego's hold over our emotions we are effectively separated from a source of higher interior guidance that would direct us toward our wholeness and fulfillment. Without the availability of that source of higher guidance we are dependent for direction on the conscious mind. The conscious mind, unfortunately, is connected to nothing more substantial than the ego. It does not see the big picture. As a result the decisions we make when we are lead by our ego may not be in our best interests.

For example, our actions may strengthen the unconscious reality system. Ruth's decisions certainly did. Or, we may deny an external source of truth we cannot countenance because it opens us to fear and insecurity. In either event, we are not moving forward. Instead we are spending our energy running in place, protecting a position that does not serve our growth or make us happy.

When the ego is dominant we use up our energy maintaining the fragmentation of the psyche. It should not be forgotten that we live in a Duality System whose prime characteristics include movement and change. Movement creates opportunity for growth. Unfortunately, the priority of a psychic system dominated by the ego tilts toward maintenance of the psyche's status quo and away from movement and growth. Consequently, the ego does not move in harmony with the nature of the duality system. Instead it moves in opposition to it. Movement and growth are its enemies. The ego does not want us to heal. It is the antagonist in the great drama of the psyche. It knows that if we succeed in becoming whole it will die.

Over time the ego learned to make a simple calculation. It realized that the more fear it could create the more power in the psyche it would accumulate. Fear was the key to its power. The real truth is a different matter. The less fear we bury and continue to experience the more whole we will be. The ego was originally brought on board to be a manager and report to us. Instead the ego has ended up a tyrant, beholden to no one, craftily using our fears against us to keep itself in power. Our job is to destroy the roots of the ego by consciously confronting the buried trauma in the psyche that give it sustenance and energy. The ego will finally die when we complete the T Zone experience and close the gaps in the psyche.

# CHAPTER SEVEN

## The Three Levels of the Will

The conscious will is a powerful instrument that can help us attain success in the material world. Its strength is best utilized in action that moves forward and outward. Since the conscious will is action oriented it is an important tool for mastering the horizontal scale of life.

For example, if our goal was to be a writer we would have to discipline ourselves to write on a regular basis, preferably every day for a specific period of time. Discipline, or doing what is needed to do to achieve success, is an important quality of the conscious will. In every successful activity of the conscious will, available energy is linked to a plan of action so that one's conscious intention can be manifested. It is the responsibility of the conscious will to fuse energy, action and intention into a specifically directed, singular force so that progress can be made toward our goals. It is the conscious will's fusion of these three necessary ingredients that provides the power to actualize many of our dreams.

However, when we shift our focus from the horizontal to the vertical scale and begin the search for inner fulfillment we reach an area of life where the conscious will has considerably less operating power than it does in the material world. This is because inner fulfillment is not so much about striving after a goal and making a plan to get there, as it is about emptying oneself of conflict, and letting go of one's demands on life.

Thus, when we shift our attention to the vertical scale we use a different aspect of the will to make the ascent to higher consciousness. This aspect of the will is the consecrated will of the spirit. The higher will of the spirit originates outside of the time zone. It belongs to eternity and by its nature is an agent of peace, accepting all things as they are. The conscious will, on the other hand, belongs strictly in the time zone. It is restless and critical, wanting to change the way things are, believing that change brings improvement. While this is often true, it is not always true. For example, if we were to move into a bigger house in a more prestigious neighborhood the change in circumstances should make us feel happier and more fulfilled. But if we left behind all our friends and extended family to move into an area where people were cooler and emotionally more distant it might make us feel isolated, lonely and depressed instead. Despite the nature of the conscious will, external change and improvement do not necessarily translate into inner fulfillment.

The higher will pursues a different course than the conscious will because it has a special knowledge that the conscious will lacks. Its advantage in relationship to the conscious will is that it partakes of Divine wisdom while the conscious will does not. As a result of this connection to the Oneness the consecrated will knows that when we accept people and circumstances as they are, giving unconditional love to each person and each situation, events will shift and change in their own rhythm as people and situations evolve towards their positive potential. The unconditional love that flows from the Oneness puts things in right order. The consecrated will is the instrument through which unconditional love flows into the time zone and enters this world. While the conscious will is impatient, wanting to achieve its goals immediately through force the consecrated will is patient, waiting for the right moment to create the right order of events so that what was once only potential and perhaps unseen may finally be realized. Patience, timing, and right order come from a connection to the Oneness, not from within the confines of the time zone itself. That connection is the special dispensation of the consecrated will.

There is nothing wrong with the conscious will's singular focus on improving one's circumstances, of course. It is an important aspect of life. The point is that improvement should not be confused with fulfillment. They belong to different realms of being. Improvement is external. Fulfillment is internal. To achieve the first does not mean we have attained the second. A change in circumstances can be rewarding. A change in consciousness is transforming. Transformation means we have increased our inner light, closed gaps in our psyche, and made progress in the vertical ascent. A change in circumstances alone will not close the gaps in our psyche.

Carl Jung put the dichotomy between striving after things and finding inner fulfillment this way. "The man whose interests are all outside is never satisfied with what is necessary, but is perpetually hankering after more and better which, true to his bias, he always seeks outside himself. He forgets completely that, for all his outward successes, he himself remains the same inwardly . . . To be satiated with "necessities" is no doubt an inestimable source of happiness, yet the inner man continues to raise his claim, and this can be satisfied by no outward possessions. And the less this voice is heard in the chase after the brilliant things of this world, the more the inner man becomes the source of inexplicable misfortune and uncomprehended unhappiness in the midst of living conditions whose outcome was expected to be entirely different. The externalization of life turns to incurable suffering, because no one can understand why he should suffer from himself. No one wonders at his insatiability, but regards it as his lawful right, never thinking that the one-sidedness of this psychic diet leads in the end to the gravest disturbances of equilibrium."

If we can learn how to activate the consecrated higher will we won't be subjected to the "incurable suffering" described by Jung. The voice of the consecrated will is the voice of our destiny. This voice speaks in the silence and is only heard when the normal chatter of the mind has ceased. The voice of the consecrated will is the intuition. When the mind is quiet and the negative content of the unconscious has been cleared the inner voice of the intuition can make its presence felt. When we are able to listen to this inner voice we can resolve many of our dilemmas, find our way through difficult situations, and move towards fulfilling our true calling and destiny. When we listen *and* act on the intuition we are in a state of surrender, allowing something higher than the mind and ego to guide us through life.

Once, my dog got out of the backyard and wandered away through the neighborhood. A busy street was close by and I was worried that she would get killed or stolen. When I realized she was gone I bolted out of the front door in a panic to begin searching for her. I had no idea which way she had gone so I ran down the street calling her name.

After several minutes of fruitless search I finally burned the franticness out of my system. My mind became still and very clear. At that moment my intuition kicked in and I got a strong feeling that I should go home and wait. That seemed sort of silly because she wasn't home, but what I was doing wasn't working either. So I suspended my doubt about what I was feeling and went home and waited. A few minutes later there was a knock on the door. It was a young boy who lived a few doors up the street in the opposite direction from the one I had taken to search for my dog.

"Do you have a small, black dog with gold eyebrows and a gold star on her chest?" he asked.

"Yes I do."

"She's in my front yard. I thought you'd want to know."

"I do. That's great. Thanks for telling me. I'll be right over to get her." In that moment I was very glad that I had listened to the feeling in my solar plexus rather than the doubt in my reasoning mind.

My original plan in searching for my dog failed. This original plan was an action of the conscious will, fusing energy, with a plan, and an intention. The problem with this plan was I went the wrong way. The conscious will can be an effective instrument but it is also an incomplete mechanism for getting us where we need to go in life. This is because the conscious will can as easily lead us in the wrong direction as it can lead us in the right one. In contrast, the higher consecrated will of the spirit always shows us the right way.

The thing we have to learn is how to first locate and then activate the higher will. The key to locating the consecrated will is to remember that the level of the will we are able to utilize is determined by the level of consciousness we have attained. The door to the higher will opens when we make the vertical ascent, not before. Until we make that ascent our consciousness is limited by the gaps in our psyche. If we don't take the time and go to the trouble of making ourselves whole the consecrated will can't function in our lives. Instead we will be limited to the time zone and the horizontal scale, forced to rely on only the conscious will to get what we want.

My intuition came to my aid again when I was looking for a house in Los Angeles. I had been looking for a place to live for over two months with no success. I had tried newspaper listings, realtors and special agencies. All the normal roads led nowhere. I was feeling very frustrated. Then one day I "got" the idea to drive around a Santa Monica neighborhood I had recently discovered and see if I might find a place that would work for me.

I decided to use my intuition in this search. My plan was simple. At each intersection I would stop for a second or two and listen internally for the direction I should go in. Should I go straight, turn left, or turn right? I decided I would go in the direction I felt drawn toward. I had nothing to lose and so did this experiment for awhile. Soon I found myself weaving through an area that I had never been in before. Finally, after about twenty minutes of driving through this area I arrived in front of a house with a for rent sign in the front yard. The house was on a lovely street. It seemed clean and in excellent condition.

I went to the front door and rang the bell. As luck would have it, the owner was inside showing it to a woman who seemed very interested in renting it. He told me I might as well come in and look around too. He continued on, engrossed in his discussion with the woman and ignored me. My intuition told me not to worry, that the woman would soon leave, and the house was mine to rent. A few minutes later the woman left and the owner and I began a conversation. It was soon obvious to both of us that we had a lot in common. I rented the house that afternoon. During that initial conversation the owner told me that he had just put up the For Rent sign a few hours before. Some weeks later, after I moved in, he told me that in the following two days after he had rented the house to me he received more than seventy inquiries from other parties wanting to lease the house.

If I hadn't followed my intuition that day from deciding to go to that neighborhood, to letting my intuition lead me through its streets, to waiting for the woman to leave, I never would have found that house. My timing was perfect and involved a complex series of steps that seemed simple at the time it was happening. I didn't have a chance to think. Everything just flowed the way it should. That sense of flow is an attribute of the higher will. The house proved to be in a great neighborhood. It was safe, clean and the people on the block were warm and friendly. I made many good friends on that street and my son had lots of children his age to play with. My intuition waited until the perfect moment before it prompted me to go to that neighborhood. I had already been looking for a home for more than two months without success. If I had gone the day before the sign would not have been out. If I had gone a day later the property would have already been rented. My intuition arranged everything so that my actions coincided with the right timing of events. What seemed like blind luck was really already planned from somewhere above. All I had to do was follow my intuition to get there.

## The Involuntary Will

So far we have discussed the will of the conscious mind and the consecrated will of the higher mind or spirit. But they are only two of the three aspects of the will. The third aspect of the will is the involuntary will of the unconscious mind. We have discussed the involuntary will to some extent in previous chapters. The major concern of the involuntary will is its consistent ability to sabotage the successful implementation of either the will of the conscious mind or the consecrated will of the higher mind. As long as the involuntary will is operating it is the dominant aspect of the will. It can block the path to success or create a chasm in the psyche that cannot be crossed in the pursuit of inner fulfillment.

The involuntary will is able to override the intentions of the two other components of the will because the will is not a monolithic or unified attribute of consciousness while the psyche is fragmented. In a very real sense, the state of the psyche determines the state of the will. If the psyche is fragmented the will is segmented. A segmented will makes it very difficult to manifest the conscious plans and goals of the individual because the tendency of the involuntary will of the unconscious is to work in opposition to the desire and intent of the conscious will. Until the psyche is healed the involuntary will has its own separate agenda, which it will pursue with determination and resolve.

A client of mine was severely beaten by her stepfather when she was just a year old. When she was a teenager she was raped by an acquaintance. As an adult her relationships with men have been disastrous. Her pattern in relationships is to seduce men into a commitment through sex. But once a man commits himself to her she punishes him by first cutting off the sex and then pushing him away. This pattern is very troubling and disturbing to her because consciously she wants a good, supportive, loving relationship. Unfortunately, the pattern that controls her behavior is self-destructive. Instead of a loving relationship she is constantly punishing men and being unhappy with herself for doing so. Until recently she had no idea why she has been compelled to hurt men rather than love them.

This client has also been in conventional therapy for some time and never has revealed or discussed the rape with her therapist. The reason for her nondisclosure is that she has buried the rape so deeply inside herself that she forgot it ever happened. When she lay down on my healing table for her second session I could see the energy of that rape all over her hips and pelvic region. It was so obvious to me that I asked her in a very sensitive fashion if she had ever been sexually abused. As soon as I asked her the question she burst into tears. At that moment the unresolved emotional energy in her system was finally mobilized and the grief and rage came pouring out of her. She cried and screamed for the rest of that session.

The next week she came to my office, lay down on my table again, and said resignedly, "I guess I hate men. I guess that's why I keep hurting them."

"I don't know that you hate all men," I replied. "But you hate the man who beat you over nothing when you were a year old and you hate the man who raped you when you were a teenager. That's normal, given what has happened to you. Unfortunately, what your unconscious has concluded from your experiences is that all men are bad and all men will hurt you. Therefore as soon as you let someone get close to you these internalized beliefs propel the personal reality system of your involuntary will into automatic overdrive and you start your retreat from commitment, pursuing a two pronged attack strategy as you do so. First you push these men out of your life and then you punish them for the past actions of other men. In your unconscious you decided long ago that men must pay for hurting you. But while you make them pay you continue to pay as well. You don't get what you want either. Men victimized you but now you are the victim of your own subjective truth. Our subjective truth is often self-destructive and controls our reality without our being aware of it. Your perception of the truth, not the truth itself, has created this situation. The objective truth is different from your perceived truth. Not all men are bad. The objective truth is that while some men are bad most men are good and decent. You have the power and intelligence as an adult to find one that will be supportive and respectful and treat you well. But you will never be able to shift your life upward to use that power until you heal yourself of the psychic scars you carry from the past. Your involuntary will must be emptied of all this hidden trauma. Until that happens your personal reality system will activate automatically and destroy your relationships."

"Oh God," she replied. "I feel so hopeless. Can I ever change this pattern? I want to have a normal life. And I want to have some happiness."

"You are changing it. That's what this work is all about. Last week you consciously reconnected with and confronted the rape. All the buried, repressed emotion of that trauma rose to the surface from where it had been stored in your hips and pelvis. As you expressed that energy through sobbing, screaming, kicking and raging you processed out a great deal of it. When the rest of that buried emotion is discharged from your system it will no longer have any power in your unconscious reality system. The objective truth will replace your subjective truth and you will have the power to create what you consciously want. When you have your healing you won't be a prisoner of your limiting beliefs, automatically self-destructing and destroying what you want. But while you're healing and processing out all that heavy emotion it's only normal to feel hopeless, depressed and powerless. Weren't those emotions part of your unexpressed response to the trauma you suffered when you were a child and a teenager? And didn't you bury those feelings because you had no way to deal with them?"

"Yes. I guess I did."

"So the fact that you're feeling them so intently now only means that they have finally come to the surface where you can do something about them. These feelings indicate that you're moving forward and healing yourself. In the transformation process you must go into your powerless and hopelessness before you can have your power back and find happiness. You are well on your way. But first you had to become conscious of the repressed events that were giving the involuntary will of your unconscious so much power. The more disconnected you are from the buried events that have disrupted your life the more power the involuntary will of the unconscious has to continue disrupting your life even more, destroying your personal power and self-esteem."

## The Covert Nature of the Involuntary Will

As this case clearly shows, it is dangerous to leave the involuntary will of the unconscious in control because both it's content and it's workings are hidden from conscious sight. This lack of observation, or oversight, permits the involuntary will to work in a dark psychic obscurity where it remains unchecked and unchallenged. It is only when we bring this hidden content out of its obscurity and up to the surface that we can successfully challenge and overcome it. Until we do so the involuntary will of the unconscious dominates our life.

## Our Greatest Opponent

The greatest opponent any of us will ever face then is the buried emotional content of the unconscious will. This buried content is the source of our undoing. The enemy we fear most is not outside us but sits in the shadows of our psyche.

The T Zone is the place where we turn and stand face to face with the hidden contents of the involuntary will. This confrontation stirs up all the fear, grief, rage and terror we have buried in our souls throughout the centuries. When this content is finally exposed to the healing light, the energy that feeds and empowers the negative personal reality system of the unconscious can be readily discharged. The whole purpose of the T Zone experience is to take back our power from what we fear and make ourselves more whole and conscious. If we succeed in this endeavor we will move forward and upward on the vertical scale, earning the right to have a more rewarding and fulfilling life experience.

## The Paradox of Transformation

Until we have transformed the emotional material buried in our bodies the conscious mind and will has no power over the involuntary will of the unconscious. That is why the language of transformation is highly paradoxical. The way up to the light is the way down into the darkness. The path to power and wholeness begins in powerlessness, despair and fragmentation. The stairway to heaven climbs upward from the steps of hell. If we want to climb higher we must start at the beginning. In the T Zone we embrace the darkness hidden in the unconscious side of the psyche so we can experience the Light that shines in the core of our being. We move through what is untrue so we can find our real truth. There is no other way.

## Transforming an Enemy into an Ally

When the hidden content of the involuntary will is cleared and emptied, it is no longer our opponent but becomes our ally. At this point it is much easier to move towards our goals because the unconscious is free to lend its immense power to creating what we desire, rather than recreating what we don't want. With the resolution of buried emotional content the psyche comes back to balance and wholeness.

The balance achieved between the unconscious and conscious sides of the psyche is the foundation for the consecrated, higher will of the spirit. The higher spiritual aspect of the will cannot come into play until the lower, involuntary will of the unconscious is emptied and cleared of its negative content. Thus, the problem posed by the negative content of the involuntary will must be resolved before one's spiritual development can proceed.

### Eleven Important Points about the Involuntary Will

Let us now summarize what we have learned about the operation and function of the involuntary will of the unconscious.

1. The involuntary will functions *automatically* and *independently* of the conscious mind and will.

2. The will of the unconscious *repeats* the suffering and pain of the past. As long as buried emotional content resides in the unconscious the involuntary will is the *power* in our lives. This means that the past will be prologue to the future.

3. The involuntary will of the unconscious prevents what we consciously want from happening. Its ongoing activity represents a covert form of *self-sabotage*.

4. The involuntary will keeps us *fragmented* and *powerless*, deepening the gaps in our being. While the

involuntary will is operative we cannot be whole.

5. The involuntary will keeps us *disconnected* from spirit and therefore unable to access our intuitive guidance to any great extent. While the involuntary will is active we cannot be enlightened.

6. The involuntary will of the unconscious *interferes* with our growth and evolution. Instead of moving up the vertical scale with momentum and speed we move haltingly at a snails pace, if we move at all. The will of the unconscious makes our growth, evolution and spirituality *questionable*. Such is *its* power.

7. The good news is that we have the power to undo the hold of the involuntary will over our lives. Such is *our* power.

8. In order to exercise that power we must *choose* to enter the negative gate of the spiritual path and confront the hidden darkness and shadows in our psyche. The place of confrontation with the hidden contents of the unconscious is the T Zone.

9. The T Zone is the path to psychic wholeness as well as the door to what lies beyond wholeness, spiritual enlightenment.

10. To reach for one's highest destiny is a deliberate conscious choice. To surrender to one's fate and

remain ensnared in the miasma of the involuntary will is also a deliberate, if unconscious choice. The ultimate question we all face is which path shall we choose, the path that rises in the light or the path that sinks in the darkness. No one can choose for us, but us.

11. **Consciousness is not an accident**. It is a choice.

The T Zone is the place where we turn and stand face to face with the hidden contents of the involuntary will. This confrontation stirs up all the fear, grief, rage and terror we have buried in our souls throughout the centuries. When this content is finally exposed to the healing light, the energy that feeds and empowers the negative personal reality system of the unconscious can be readily discharged. The whole purpose of the T Zone experience is to take back our power from what we fear and make ourselves more whole and conscious. If we succeed in this endeavor we will move forward and upward on the vertical scale, earning the right to have a more rewarding and fulfilling life experience.

# CHAPTER EIGHT

## Forgiveness

The healing process is not complete without forgiving those who have hurt us. Forgiveness is the logical outcome, the last step in discharging the negative content in the psyche. If we look at forgiveness as part of a process rather than as a distinct and separate act, we realize that forgiveness is not in itself a choice but rather the inevitable result of making the right choice. The act of forgiveness can neither be willed nor forced because we can not forgive those who caused us harm until we first have released all the hurt that harm has caused us.

When we have discharged all of our negative emotional content, forgiveness comes naturally and easily. It is not something we have to do but something we want to do. Otherwise forgiveness is an act of will, something we force on ourselves from the outer layers of the mind, where the psyche interacts with the external world, rather than a process that moves troubling emotional content up and out from the depths of the psyche. It is dangerous to try to force our will on the psyche from the outside because it means we are attempting to move in a direction that is not in harmony with the internal functions of the psyche. The psyche will respond to our orders and demands by creating an internal rebellion, the outcome of which will be far removed from the result we originally intended.

Let's say, for example, that Tim and Bob had been best friends for years. Then Tim stole fifty dollars from Bob. Bob didn't learn about the theft for some weeks and only found out about it because Tim told a mutual friend in confidence about what he had done. That friend came forward and told Bob what had happened. Naturally, Bob was furious. His anger wasn't so much about the money. He would have given Tim the money if he had asked for it. His anger was about the breach of trust. He knew that breach could never be repaired. Tim had betrayed him. Their friendship was over. Bob decided that the only thing he could do was to forgive Tim and move on. So he went to church, prayed and forgave Tim. He felt good about it for a few days. Then he found himself getting inexplicably angry and wanting to beat Tim to pieces. Bob was perplexed. He had forgiven Tim. Why was he feeling this way?

Bob was angry because he had tried to force forgiveness on his psyche. Within a few days his unconscious responded to his prayers for forgiveness by throwing up the real feelings he had not dealt with in any meaningful way. In this instance Bob's psyche refused to either cooperate with his conscious will or collude in his dishonesty toward his real feelings. Instead his psyche rebelled and showed Bob the truth of the matter.

In dealing with the psyche it is always best to do first things first. If we wish to be free enough to forgive those who harmed us we have to first face, feel and discharge our anger and hurt. There is no real escape from the feelings buried in the psyche. They must be faced if we wish to move forward with our lives. The purpose of the T Zone is to uncover and heal the dark realities buried in the psyche so we can create a better reality in our lives.

### The Implicit Danger in the Notion of Forgive and Forget

The popular notion that has been perpetuated for centuries about forgiveness is that we should "forgive and forget." Implicit in this assumption is the idea that forgiveness is a form of self-sacrifice. In this view, the practice of forgiveness means that we should be big enough to forget what happened and permit the perpetrator who caused us considerable pain to be allowed back into our lives. Sometimes this practice is the sensible thing to do. For instance, I will forgive my son anything. He's young and bound to make mistakes. Besides, there's not a mean bone in his body. But "forgive and forget" is not always the wise thing to do. It depends on who has hurt us.

Let's say that I was involved in a relationship with someone who was verbally and emotionally abusive on a consistent basis. This person's behavior caused me a great deal of pain, robbed me of my self-esteem and diminished my sense of personal power. I worked very hard to forgive him. But as soon as I forgave this person, he repeated the same abusive behavior. Nothing had changed. My forgiveness work had not resolved anything except that it had encouraged my abuser to continue to abuse me. He perceived my forgiveness of him as a sign of weakness. And he was right.

### Forgiveness and Self-Sacrifice

"Forgive and forget" keeps us in harm's way when it is practiced on the wrong kind of person. This kind of self-sacrifice is not warranted and is rarely appropriate. It is forgiveness without boundaries and without self-respect. It robs us of our self-esteem, undermines our personal power and encourages an ongoing sense of helplessness. It changes nothing. The same patterns will continue. Forgiveness as self-sacrifice is neither helpful nor noble. It does not put us on a higher level than our opponent. All thoughts to the contrary are illusionary in nature, nothing but the rationalizations of weakness. Moreover, since the practice of "forgive and forget" fails to either empower us or free us from the past, it means that we will not have the power we need to make the vertical ascent, and find our wholeness. There is nothing practical, or spiritual about this form of forgiveness.

The following four points are a summary list of the major problems in the practice of "forgive and forget":

1. The policy of "forgive and forget" is self-sacrificing. It diminishes our self-esteem and personal power.

2. Nothing changes through the practice of "forgive and forget". The same destructive behavior continues.

3. "Forgive and forget" does not put us on a higher level than our opponent. It simply makes us vulnerable to receiving more blows.

4. The practice of "forgive and forget" prevents us from making the vertical ascent.

### Forgive and Remember

A wiser course in the practice of forgiveness is to "forgive and remember". When we forgive and remember we are able to set effective boundaries and empower ourselves. For instance, if someone abuses me I will forgive that person. I will process and discharge all my negative emotion so I can reach forgiveness. But I will also make sure, to the best of my abilities, that this individual never has an opportunity to abuse me again. He will not be allowed back into my life because he has shown me what he is capable of. My boundary regarding abuse is very simple. "Use me or abuse me, and you lose me."

## Forgiveness and Anger

The main reason I forgive those who hurt me is so that I won't carry anger towards them in my psyche. If I do hold onto anger I hurt myself in several ways. First, the anger I allow to get stuck in my system severs my connection to the Oneness, festers in my unconscious and creates a gap in my psyche. Second, if I carry this anger in my system I am vulnerable to being attacked by other similarly abusive people. My repressed anger will bring me down to their level where I will be open to receiving their blows. Buried anger will not protect me. Instead it will expose me to more harm.

In contrast, forgiveness permits me to be centered and connected to the Oneness. That connection allows love to flow into me and through me. That love is unconditional, impersonal, sustaining and supportive. Impersonal love allows us to love our enemies and those who have hurt us. But it doesn't mean we have to personally like them. Liking someone is a personal choice. Forgiveness returns us to the impersonal state where we can love and be whole, no matter what. That is our entire obligation. We don't have to like those who have hurt us or let them back in our life, just love them and let them go in love. But we do need to set effective boundaries when we forgive. We don't want the past repeated.

If I persist in holding onto my anger it *ties me indefinitely* to the person who made me angry. Anger that is unacknowledged and repressed creates a karmic relationship. Karmic relationships are unpleasant, debilitating and repetitive. When we fail to deal with a traumatic situation we will experience that situation over and over again. Remember the words of Lao Tzu, "Because the sage confronts his difficulties he never experiences them." The failure to confront our anger and the practice of "forgive and forget" both lead to the same inevitable result. Negative situations continue, personal power is diminished and self-esteem is destroyed.

To forgive and remember is not self-sacrificial like the practice of "forgive and forget". Rather it is self-affirming. We forgive those who trespass against us for the advantages that forgiving them brings to us. When we forgive and set effective boundaries we take back our power and increase our self-esteem.

### Forgiveness and Freedom

No one has the right to abuse us. Abuse in any form is intolerable and unacceptable. To forgive and permit abuse to occur or reoccur in our life is a potent form of self-denial and lack of self-respect. We forgive to increase our strength and autonomy, not to lose our power and continue our enslavement to those who would bind us to them. When we forgive in the right way we cut our ties to the past and are no longer its slave. We emerge from forgiveness whole and psychically intact, ready to embark on an entirely new course in life.

### Forgiveness and Self-Love

To forgive and remember is an act of Self-love. Self-love is not narcissistic because it does not induce self-involvement. We are not preoccupied with our dilemmas. Quite the contrary; we are able put ourselves aside, enjoy life and help others. The T Zone is a place of deep alchemy where the old life dies and a new one emerges from the depths of our hidden darkness. What comes out of the T Zone is always wider, deeper and more enriching than the old life was. We walk through the fire to rise in the Light. Forgiveness is the moment in the process when we finally cross the threshold and emerge in that Light.

The following points are a summary of the major advantages in the practice of "Forgive and Remember":

1. The practice of "Forgive and Remember" enables us to set effective boundaries, increase our self-esteem, and enhance our personal power.

2. It permits us to be centered and connected with the Oneness.

3. It releases the past and opens the door to the future.

4. It allows us to be an instrument of unconditional love.

# CHAPTER NINE

## Twelve True Tales from the T Zone

The cycle of miracles begins when we turn and confront the trauma buried in our bodies. In that moment we enter the T Zone and the process of becoming conscious commences.

## 1

Miriam grew up in Europe. She was born after her father went off to war and did not actually meet him until she was nearly three years old. When her father came home from the war she quickly became his favorite. He took her with him everywhere.

Unfortunately, this angered her mother a great deal. Her own parents had emotionally abandoned her when she was a child. Now her husband was neglecting her. Her childhood nightmare was happening all over again. It was too much for her to take. She blamed Miriam for her husband's lack of attention. When she had been a child she had been helpless to change things and get her needs met. Now she was an adult and had the power to do something about it. She came up with a novel and cruel solution.

When Miriam was five her mother sent her to live in a Catholic orphanage. Suddenly Miriam had no family. It was her turn to be twisted, destroyed and heartbroken by the pathological dysfunction within her family system. The pattern of abandonment that had begun in the previous generation was still operating in Miriam's family. Only in this iteration of the pattern the virulence expressed by Miriam's mother toward her was more intense and devastating than the neglect displayed by Miriam's grandmother toward her mother had been.

This pattern illustrates an important point that I have touched on previously in this book. Time doesn't necessarily make things better. If emotional trauma isn't effectively dealt with at the time it occurs then it is all too likely that the future repercussions of that trauma will be of a greater intensity than the original incident.

When Miriam came to see me she was suffering from chronic back pain in the mid-thoracic region. She sensed that there were hidden emotional issues that needed to be addressed, but she hadn't been able to connect to them in any conscious fashion. Instead the feeling of emotional turmoil lingered in the background, just outside the periphery of her knowing. The first time she came in I put my hand immediately on the part of her back where her pain was located.

"It hurts here," I said.

"Yes," she replied.

"This has to do with your mother."

"Oh?" she said, with a trace of anxiety in her voice.

I let the healing energy flow into her for awhile then when I felt the time was right I asked her to make a sound, any sound she wanted, as if it was coming out of that part of her back. She began by making sounds like "uhhh!" and "ohhh!" At first it required a lot of effort on her part. She was very self-conscious and felt foolish doing this in front of me.

As we began our work together, I explained to her that transformational healing does not take place on a rational, verbal level. It takes place on an emotional and energetic level. First we have to locate where the emotional content is buried and then we must consciously connect to the feelings and memories buried there. If we don't first "find and feel" the buried emotional content little will happen. In Miriam's case we were already half way there. We had found the place in her body where much of her buried material was stored. Once she was able to connect her consciousness to the blocked energy in her body the healing process would be activated, becoming natural and automatic. Instead of forcing herself to make sounds, the sounds of her trauma would flow out of the buried spaces in her body in their own way and at their own speed.

Initially it took a fair amount of work on her part to make conscious contact with the site of the buried emotional material in her body. Her initial difficulty was due to the fact that the trauma had been frozen in her body long ago. This is a fairly common occurrence. She was emotionally numb and had forgotten much of her childhood. "Numbing out" had been the only way she could cope and survive with the enormity of the emotional disaster that had been visited upon her.

While going numb is a short-term solution to the problem of survival it has serious long-term consequences. It will get us through childhood. It will not get us through the rest of our life. Going numb means we shut ourselves down emotionally and split off a part of ourselves so that we can endure and go on.

*When we downshift into the "survive and endure" mode we have chosen to remain unconscious and disconnected from our wholeness. The price we will pay for our unconsciousness will be the failure of our life to fulfill its promise and potential. If we decide not to strive for consciousness we choose instead to conspire against ourselves, becoming the chief agent in our self-destruction.*

The only answer to the ongoing problem of family dysfunction and psychic wounding is the healing of consciousness. Miriam is in a no win situation. She is left with her pain and the certainty that she will create more suffering for herself, dragging her past with her, like a shadow that never sleeps, wherever she goes. Her only hope for real change is to enter the T Zone and heal her consciousness.

In her second session Miriam had a breakthrough. After several minutes of forced effort in making the sounds, she consciously connected with the pain in her back. Conscious contact with hidden trauma is a form of psychic ignition. It starts the engine of healing. For Miriam, the content of her buried pain started coming up on its own. She no longer had to work on it. The process had reversed itself. It was now working on her. At first she cried a little and moaned softly. Then she sobbed and screamed out her grief and anger for the rest of that session.

In the next several sessions all I had to do was touch that spot in her back, let the healing energy flow into her and within a few moments the grief would come up on its own accord and she would sob for a long time. As the buried content was dislodged the memories of her childhood surfaced. After a wave of grief had passed and Miriam had stopped her sobbing she would speak to me about the old memories that were coming up. She remembered events from childhood that had been fully forgotten and saw the connection between her mother's betrayal and the important relationships in her own life where she too had been reaching for love and was rejected.

It was a shock when she realized that the older girl in the orphanage she had befriended and looked up to as a mother figure for many years was just like her mother. She was cold, distant and critical. Later when they were both adults and long gone from the orphanage she too betrayed Miriam.

Both of Miriam's husbands also had been cold, distant and emotionally unavailable. Her first husband stole her son's inheritance. The second husband stole her money. They used her, never saw who she was, and never respected the tremendous inner strength and humanity that shone like a star in her eyes. It had been her fate to attract people into her life who should have seen who she was and supported and loved her but instead demeaned and tried to destroy her. The miracle of Miriam was that despite all the abuse she suffered it never killed her essential nature. She was very warm, with a big heart and a great capacity for loving. She just didn't get love back in return.

The reason she could never attract love into her life was that after her mother had betrayed and abandoned her as a child she had subconsciously concluded that she must be a bad person and therefore unworthy of being loved. This belief activated her personal reality system and attracted people into her life who would never love her. Her subjective truth was destroying her life.

As we continued working the grief proceeded to pour out of her. It now flowed in torrents like a swollen river breaking through a dam. Within a few weeks of her participation in The Beacon Program she reported that her back felt much better. Most of the pain was gone. By the time she completed her tenth session she was a different person. Her eyes shone with a clarity and brightness that had not been there before. The stress was out of her face and she knew where she was going in the future. Most importantly, there was a bright light and sense of power radiating from her that indicated she had gone a long way toward integrating her psyche and taking back her power from where it had been split off and buried in her body. During the program she had quickened her evolution and made significant progress in the vertical ascent.

### The Problem of Human Love

While Miriam's story is personal and therefore unique it also illustrates a larger dilemma that effects all of us. It is the problem of human love. Most people grow up in dysfunctional family situations. Dysfunction occurs when one's emotional needs aren't met. Parents in most dysfunctional family systems don't get along and as a result many children don't receive the nurturing, validation and acceptance they need. Because their childhood needs weren't met many people suffer from low self-esteem and are incapable of real love as adults.

Unfortunately, a child growing up in a dysfunctional situation often won't know what love is. But the wounded inner child inside the psyche will still be searching for love as an adult. There is a great deal of danger in the search for love because the wounded inner child is always attracted to the same qualities in its choice of romantic partners as those qualities in the parent(s) that originally wounded the child. As a result the wounded inner child syndrome recreates the codependent drama of childhood in adult romantic relationships. These relationships are not really about love, but about getting childhood needs met. The wounded inner child is demanding, narcissistic and self involved.

Codependent relationships are power struggles. When we are less than whole our emotional life is focussed on the desperate search for love. The focus of the codependent struggle is the attempt by each party to control their partner in a losing battle to get their needs met. No one wins in codependent relationships because the available energy is quickly used up and each partner soon grows disenchanted and unhappy.

## Why Love Never Saves

Codependent relationships then are not about love, but wear the illusion of love. Instead of having a healthy relationship with genuine love, respect and acceptance the main concern of a codependent relationship is my childhood needs versus your childhood needs. In codependent romance each partner expects love to save them, i.e. meet all their emotional needs. But love never saves anyone. That notion is a myth and an illusion. The truth is that it is wholeness, not love that saves. And wholeness is something we must find on our own for ourselves. Love will not make us whole, but wholeness will make us loving.

## Romantic Intoxication

Codependent romance is a form of intoxication. It is a subtle process that imprisons us in a relationship, or in a series of relationships, that not only do not serve our growth but keep us chained where we are, feeding the infantile needs of someone else while trying to get our needs met at the same time. This process drains us of the limited energy we possess to move forward in our own growth. Life is too short for this type of self-sacrifice. Nevertheless, in our society codependency is the norm rather than the anomaly.

The secret of consciousness is that love is not out there. The belief that the love we need exists outside ourselves is the very essence of the codependent trap. The love we all seek is inside us. The road home to love begins when we turn and face the personal contents of the unconscious where we have buried all the unloved and unloving pieces of our lives. It is in that moment that we have the chance to heal our pain and make ourselves whole. In the T Zone we have the opportunity to overcome the shadow that never sleeps. Whether we do or not is entirely up to us.

# 2

Some years ago I received a phone call from a man who had heard me speak at Michigan State University in E. Lansing, Michigan. A bad back had plagued him for over a decade. Chiropractors, M.D.'s, physical therapists, and massage therapists had been unable to help him. He called me at my office in Austin and asked if I might be able to help him. He said that he was very skeptical but he had been impressed with what he had heard during the lecture and felt when I shared the healing energy with the members of the audience. "What the hell," he said. "I'm in a lot of pain. At the very least, what I saw you do warrants a phone call."

I told him I had no idea if I could help him or not. I could promise him nothing. But I would give him everything I had. He decided to try it out and we set up a phone consultation for the next week. He called me at the appointed time and after some preliminary conversation I started sending him the healing energy over the phone. Within a few minutes he could feel a great deal of warmth and a tingling sensation suffusing his entire body. He felt light, very relaxed and much better. He was so encouraged by this first session that he decided to schedule another session for the next week.

In his next session I could see, with the aid of my interior vision, where the block was in his back. There was a very concentrated piece of congested black energy lodged against his mid-thoracic vertebrae, just beneath his heart. When I zeroed in on it I said to him, "Larry, there's this piece of energy lodged against your spine in the middle of your back. I'm certain that's the cause of your problem. I'm going to focus my energy there in a minute but I also must tell you that when this stuff surfaces there's going to be a lot of intense emotion that comes up with it. This blockage is very old, centuries old I think. It has to do with medieval times and dying in a battle. When I think I've got it loosened up I'm going to ask you to make some sounds as if they were coming out of that part of your body. Just make any old sound. It should be enough to open the gate and get at whatever emotions are buried in there. When those emotions come up I think you'll find yourself wailing like a banshee and feeling a great deal of fear. But if you let yourself go with it, I think it will help your back a great deal. Are you ready? Can you handle it?"

"Yeah. Let's do it."

"O.K. Here goes." I started sending the energy over the phone to that spot in his back. After a few minutes I asked him to begin making some sounds as if they were coming out of that spot in his back. In less than a minute the stream of "ahhs" turned into uncontrolled screams. The screaming went on for quite a long time as the unconscious content that had been lodged in that site of his body came pouring up to the surface to be discharged. When it was all over Larry was exhausted, but greatly relieved.

"That was something!" he said. "I would never have believed it if I hadn't experienced it. I saw myself being killed in battle. Someone put a broadsword through me. I was right back there in it. It felt so real. I've never felt so much terror and pain. It was all right there."

"You slipped down into another level. Right where you needed to go. How do you feel now?"

"The pain in my back is all gone! I feel incredibly light. I've got to tell you that while that was happening I was burning up. My clothes are soaking wet with sweat. I'm sure I'm an inch taller."

"You well could be. That blocked energy could have easily compressed your spine. Call me in a week and let me know how you are doing."

Larry called a week later. The pain was gone. He was an inch taller.

# 3

In Rochester, N.Y. I gave a series of lectures and healing workshops in the mid-eighties. Susan came to one of
those Friday night lectures. In the second half of the
evening I projected my healing energy into the hall so
everyone could experience it and get its benefits. The next
morning at nine I was holding an all day healing workshop.
At a few minutes after nine Susan straggled through the
door. She came directly over and started talking to me
immediately. She was quite beside herself.

"I don't know what you did to me last night. That energy was very strong. I started going hot and cold at the lecture. I'd be hot for fifteen minutes then cold for another fifteen minutes. I went home and it went on like that all
night. I felt certain that someone was going to break in to
my house and kill me. I didn't sleep at all. What did you do
to me?"

I told her that she was in the middle of processing a
large piece of unconscious material and suggested that she
lie down on one of the healing tables immediately. She was
only too relieved to comply. I got three of the workshop
participants together and showed them where I wanted
them to place their hands on her body. "Don't worry," I told
them. "This room is filled with healing energy. It will flow
through you easily and automatically. I'll be back in a
minute. I think whatever is going on inside Susan will
come up very quickly."

As the healing power flowed into Susan it took her down into the level of her personal psyche where the buried trauma was stored. The healing energy had been melting this frozen material all night. The fact that she had been alternating between fifteen minute periods of burning up then fifteen minutes of freezing indicated to me that the healing energy was literally burning up the energy block in her system. That was verified by the symptom of "burning up". The sensation she had of freezing was the mass of frozen energy melting and flowing through her system. The healing energy she had experienced the previous evening was preparing her for the final piece of the healing. It had done a very good job, even if Susan did not understand what was happening to her.

Within seconds she made contact with the buried emotional material that was now very mobile and close to the surface of her consciousness. She started to scream and cry and thrash about. It went on like this for nearly forty-five minutes. Then she became very still and peaceful.

When we finished and she got off the table her clothes were drenched in sweat. She was exhausted, but felt very light and wonderful. She told me that for the last portion of her session she was suspended in a brilliant golden light and felt totally at peace and one with all of life.

"So you went into the Oneness," I said. "You're only allowed to go there you know, after you've cleared major life karma. That's great. But what were you experiencing earlier in the session?"

"As soon as they put their hands on me I started shifting into some other place and found myself in Africa. I was a young female and part of a tribe. I was being slowly mutilated as part some sort of religious sacrifice. It was very painful and scary. I'm glad its over. I feel so much better. I've never felt this kind of peace before."

Some weeks later I received a phone call from Susan. She had just been to see her health practitioner who treated illness with herbs and used iridology as her primary diagnostic tool. The health practitioner had told Susan after examining her eyes that she had never seen so much change between appointments in any of her clients eyes as she had seen in Susan's. This woman had been a health practitioner for thirty-five years. She told Susan that she had been treating her for tumors on the right side of her body but her eyes now showed no sign of those tumors whatsoever.

# 4

Marion came to see me in my office in Austin. She had been recently diagnosed with cancer of the cervix. At the start of our session I placed one hand on the base of her stomach, the other on her lower abdomen and let the healing power flow through my hands into her body. The energy was very hot. Within a few minutes Marion's face turned blue and she started rolling her head from side to side, screaming, "I can't see! I can't see!" over and over again. I asked her to take a deep breath, relax, and let her mind shift its awareness to the base of her spine where we were focusing the healing energy. She was able to do this quite easily. I then asked her to let her mind connect with whatever was going on in her body. Within a minute or two she shifted into another life, and began experiencing an event in that lifetime of great traumatic impact.

As she connected with the buried content in her pelvis she started kicking, screaming and crying. Eventually she started screaming in German. On a conscious level Marion did not know German. Yet from this level of her psyche she screamed in German for nearly an hour. Then suddenly she became quiet and peaceful. As she became peaceful the healing energy shifted from a bright red to a beautiful, bright gold. At this point Marion, like Susan and others before her, felt as if she was floating weightless in a bright golden sky. She didn't want to come back into her body and have the experience end. Later she would say that she felt more at peace and fulfilled than she had ever felt before.

When the treatment was over Marion told me what she had experienced during the body of the session. She informed me that when I suggested that she focus her mind in her pelvic region she experienced an almost immediate shift into a past lifetime. This lifetime took place in Germany. (No surprise there.) The part of that lifetime she was reliving came from WW II. The war had just ended and her husband had come home from the fighting. She was very happy to see him. He was a German general. He told her that he had hated the killing he had had to engage in. He confided to her that he had even hated killing unarmed Jews.

Unknown to him Marion had used her position as a General's wife to cover her own clandestine operation during the war. While he was killing Jews she was smuggling them out of the country. However, she felt guilty that she had operated behind his back, without his knowledge. When he had told her how he hated killing Jews, she decided to tell him her secret. She didn't want her guilt to come between them. Unfortunately, her decision turned out to be a terrible mistake.

When he heard what she had done he went out of control. He beat her, raped her, ripped out her eyes and left her to die. When the session started and she began turning blue and screaming "I can't see!" Marion was actually beginning to relive that past death experience. As the session continued and she connected more directly with the trauma that was hidden in her soul she started screaming in German and calling out to someone named Helmut. Apparently Helmut was the name of her husband.

When she left she was sure the cancer in her cervix had been healed. I insisted however that she go back to her doctor so we would know for sure what was going on. The tests showed Marion was free of cancer.

Frequently there is a tangible connection between negative emotions that are buried in the body and the manifestation of disease. Cancer is one disease that is often traced to emotional conditions. In Marion's case the cause of her cancer came from the negative emotional content of past lifetimes that had not been cleared from her system. Once that material was cleared the cancer was healed.

# 5

Andre came to a workshop I held in Illinois. When his turn came to get on the table the healing energy flowing into his psyche downshifted his consciousness to a lifetime that had occurred during the Inquisition. In that time he had been a priest accused of heresy against the church. As he lay on the table he experienced himself being tortured, racked, and finally castrated by his captors. He died in a pool of blood, swearing eternal revenge against his torturers. As he relived these distant events, he cried, sobbed and screamed. When he got off the table he felt much lighter and strangely unburdened.

He told me later that in his present lifetime he had had testicular cancer in his right testicle that had spread to the lymph nodes in his groin. He had undergone surgery and had his right testicle removed as well as the lymph nodes on the right side of his groin. Now at least, he knew where that cancer had come from. Once again there was a connection between traumatic events that occurred lifetimes ago and the present day emergence of a deadly disease.

At the lunch break Andre called his wife Maria, related his story to her, and asked her to come to the workshop. It turned out that Maria had a problem with obesity. She was always hungry and couldn't stop eating. When her time came to get on the table I showed the people who were working at her table where to place their hands on Maria's body. There was a lot of blockage in her throat, stomach and pelvis. Soon the healing energy shifted her consciousness to another level and she found herself in another lifetime as a young Indian girl in the Andes Mountains of South America. There was never enough to eat in her village and she was always hungry. She died young and the memory of not having enough food had remained in her soul. Now I had her connect with her feelings as the young Indian girl. Soon she started to cry. She cried quietly for a long time. She lay without moving as tears streamed down her cheeks. When she got up she said she felt much lighter and different inside. She shared that she didn't feel empty anymore. Two months later she called and told me she had lost thirty pounds without effort since the workshop. The weight had just fallen off her.

# 6

At a workshop in E. Lansing, Michigan a young woman came who was enrolled in medical school at Michigan State University. She had been troubled for months by constant pain in her colon. She had consulted leading medical specialists and they had found nothing. She had gone to alternative practitioners and they too had found nothing.

When she got on the healing table I showed the people at her table where to place their hands. Almost immediately she began thrashing about and screaming. I came over to work with her as soon as she shifted into the discharge mode. She continued discharging in this manner for a long time. Finally, the discharge was over and she lay back quietly with a big smile on her face. Her clothing was soaked in sweat.

A few minutes later she got up and told us what she had experienced. When the energy first went into her she said she had seen a gold ball of light at the base of her spine. The gold light had then shot up her spine and gone out the top of her head. At that point she found herself back at about nine months old. She was in a crib and her father was sexually abusing her. That's when her screaming and thrashing about started. She was reliving what had happened to her. When she finished discharging all the emotion regarding that event she became very quiet and found herself floating in a bright golden light like many of my clients have. She felt sure that she was out of her body. She told us that she had never felt so peaceful and whole and didn't want the experience of floating in the gold light to end.

I asked her how her colon felt now. She thought about it for a few seconds and realized all the pain in her colon was gone. That was on a Saturday. I ran into her again on Tuesday in the grocery store. She came up behind me and said that as soon as she walked in the store she knew that I was in there.

"And how did you know that?" I asked her.

"I could feel your energy," she said.

"How's your stomach?" I asked.

"It's great. Since the workshop I've lost twelve pounds in three days. I can't believe it! I'm not doing anything differently. I'm not dieting. Why do you think that's happened?"

"The trauma that happened to you occurred when you were nine months old. At that time much of your emotional energy was frozen. Physically, in addition to the pain that you felt in your colon, you also kept your baby fat. Now that you have released the emotional trauma the baby fat can also be released. And that's exactly what has happened."

The next night I gave another talk. Valerie, the medical student, came. During the question and answer segment she asked me what she could do about a conflict she was having with her mother. Her grandmother had died some months ago and left her house to Valerie. Valerie wanted to sell it to pay for medical school but her mother was living in it and wouldn't let her daughter claim her inheritance. Valerie was very angry and upset.

I told her that the only thing she had any power over in

the situation were her feelings toward her mother. Until she released her anger nothing would change. Her anger was "freezing" the situation. She started to argue and complain about the unfairness of it all with me. I kept telling her she wasn't a victim and only she could change how she felt towards her mother. Otherwise all her power was going in a negative direction and nothing would change. We went back and forth for a few minutes. Finally she burst into tears and cried for a few minutes. When she was done she said, "You're right. I forgive my mother. I can't really kick her out of the house. I'll have to find another way to pay for medical school."

This exchange occurred between 8:45 and 9:00 pm. When Valerie got home there was a message on her answering machine from her mother. The time of the message was 9:05 pm. In the message her mother told her that she could sell the house. Forgiveness and letting go are powerful tools for moving forward in life.

# 7

One day I received a call from a client and good friend of mine. He had invested in a biotech company whose chief medical researcher had just had a stroke. He wanted to know if I could help this doctor. His work was very valuable to this company.

We arranged to have the secretary to the president of the company go to the hospital where the Dr. had been taken and call me later on that day from his hospital room. When the call came in I had her place the phone on his chest. I could see a knot of yellowish brown energy at the bottom of his neck on the left side. I started sending the energy over the phone to that spot immediately. Early that evening the secretary called me to report that the Dr. had been feeling very restless, hot and uncomfortable internally before I worked on him. After the session he felt cool, calm and very peaceful. I worked on him long distance by phone for three weeks. I would do three or four fifteen-minute sessions a week. At the end of the three week period he got up and walked out of the hospital on his own power. He had regained the full use of his legs. The only sign of his stroke was a weakened left arm, which I had not worked on very much.

# 8

During the late eighties I received a call from a woman in Montana who suffered from agoraphobia and constipation and wanted to know if I could help her with her problems. I told her I didn't know if I could but if she wanted to work with me I would give her all I had. That's all I could promise her, I said. In fact, that's all I ever can promise anyone. I can never guarantee success. I can only give each person the best of my abilities.

She decided she wanted to work with me and made a telephone appointment to call the next week for long distance healing. When she called I told her to lay down, get comfortable and place the phone in her lap. When she had gotten herself situated I started sending the healing energy into her stomach. She started to shiver and cry almost immediately. She didn't know why, but her crying lasted the whole session and she got colder and colder as the session went on.

I told her not to worry about the sensation of cold. It was actually a very positive sign and meant that the emotional blockage in her stomach was melting. I also told her that she might feel very emotional, sad and depressed for the next few days and if she felt that way not to worry. It just meant that the healing discharge was continuing. That's a very normal and healthy reaction to the healing work.

She called a week later at the time of her next appointment and told me as we started that she had been having regular bowel movements since our session last week. Up to that point she had been severely constipated for more than twenty years. As I started to send the healing energy into her stomach area pictures started coming up to her conscious mind of events from more than thirty years ago that she had repressed and forgotten.

While she had been married to her first husband he had taken her to town one day to get her hair done. He was supposed to come back for her in an hour. He had never returned. Instead he had gone off with another woman. As the pictures came up and she consciously connected with the buried trauma she burst into tears. Her grief continued for the rest of the session.

The next week when she called for her third appointment all her grief was gone. She reported that she had been able to go out with her second husband on his boat for the first time in nearly thirty years. The agoraphobia that had imprisoned her for three decades was gone. In this final session the healing energy balanced out her emotions and filled her with a bright white light. When the session was over she felt better and more at peace than she ever had.

# 9

Sean came to see me because his girlfriend, who was a client of mine, had already paid for his session. As he explained when he walked in the door, he didn't believe I could help him, and certainly didn't think there was anything to the work I did, but he wasn't going to waste good money either. "So let's do it and get it over with," he said. "Then we can both get on with our lives."

Sean's girlfriend Nancy had sent him to me because she wanted me to help him give up drugs and chasing other women. Nancy had fallen in love with Sean and wanted him to settle down, get a real job, become respectable and be faithful to her.

"That's a tall order for one session," I had told her. "I don't think it's very likely much will change that quickly."

"I know," she said. "But I can still hope."

With his attitude the way it was I was sure nothing would happen and the session would be a waste of time. We proceeded, my doubts notwithstanding. Sean got on my healing table. I placed one hand under the base of his neck, the other under the base of his spine and let the healing energy flow through me into him. Soon Sean was very relaxed, almost sleeping. Then suddenly he started moaning. His face turned ashen gray and he began moving his head back and forth. After a few minutes of this activity he became silent and still. His eyes opened wide and he looked up very intently at the ceiling for a moment. He looked shocked by whatever it was he was seeing. Then his eyes closed. A few minutes later he started shivering and shaking. He said he was freezing and asked for a blanket. It was in the mid-nineties outside and the air conditioning in my office had only lowered the temperature to 81 degrees. It was anything but cold. I gave him a blanket, then put one hand on his spine behind his heart and the other hand on top of his chest, over his heart. A few minutes later he started sobbing. The sobs went on for the better part of an hour. After he was done crying his whole body started to vibrate and continued to do so for several minutes. Then he lay back exhausted, gray and still shivering. The session was over.

After he recovered and got up he sat on my sofa, still wrapped in the blanket and shivering slightly. "What happened?" he asked. "What was all that?"

"Tell me what you experienced."

"Well, I got relaxed then strange things started happening. I began to shake then I felt like I had to open my eyes. When I did I saw a beam of white light coming out of my forehead. The light made a cross on the ceiling. The next thing I knew I was in the desert, part of a long line of slaves dragging stones across the sand to be used to build the pyramids of Egypt. Next to the lines of slaves dragging the stones there were these overseers who were whipping people and if one of them felt some slave wasn't working hard enough he'd pull that slave out of the line and whip him severely. I know that many slaves died from the whipping. Then an overseer pulled a woman out of the line just ahead of me and whipped her to death. I couldn't show any emotion at what was going on because if I did they would have pulled me out and whipped me too."

He took a breath, and paused a moment before continuing. "That woman was my wife. I was crying for her death just now and what it did to me. I don't think I ever cried about it till now. That I can sort of understand, but why did I feel so cold and shaky?"

"The cold you felt," I answered. "Was the frozen emotional trauma buried inside your system coming to the surface and melting. While that may feel somewhat uncomfortable it's an excellent sign. It means that the trauma will no longer bind up your life and prevent you from moving forward. The vibrating you did after you stopped crying was the energy of your emotional body catching up with where you are now. It had been stuck way back in time. You'll probably have a few days where your body and consciousness will be integrating and adjusting to your healing. Don't be surprised if you're a bit tired and low for a couple of days. It's only natural after what you have been through. Let me know what happens."

I never saw or heard from Sean again. Three months later I received a call from a mutual friend of Sean and Nancy's who also was a client of mine.

"Did you hear what happened to Sean?" she asked.

"No. I've not heard anything from him."

"Amazing. He quit bartending within a week of seeing you. He got a job in sales with IBM and is doing very well at it. He also met a girl he fell in love with and is now engaged to her."

"What about Nancy?"

"He broke up with her."

"What sad irony. Everything she wanted with Sean has happened, only with another woman."

"Here's the funny part. Sean was blown away with what happened to him when he saw you. He has never been able to accept it or figure it out so he's come up with a rather novel explanation for what happened to him."

"And that is?"

"Well, he figured that you put LSD on your fingers and when you touched his feet the LSD somehow got into his bloodstream and he started tripping."

I laughed. "Now that's creative. A bit off the mark, but creative. The thing that's important to me is how his life changed so dramatically. Good for him."

The slave experience and his wife's death had been imbedded in dark regions of Sean's psyche for more than two thousand years. Because of that experience he had formed certain beliefs about his personal reality that had dominated him over the course of several lifetimes. His unconscious reality system was based on the beliefs that, "if you love someone they will die," and "if you permit yourself to be seen you might die." Consequently he had unconsciously structured his life to avoid love and commitment. He worked in dark clubs where he couldn't be easily seen. His love life consisted of a series of one night stands and he smoked dope daily to medicate his pain.

His session released the buried trauma and emotion concerning the slave lifetime of more than two thousand years ago. When he discharged his trauma he also disarmed the beliefs in his unconscious reality system. The two beliefs that had dominated him no longer had any power over him. As a result he was able to walk away from his past and into a new life.

# 10

Barbara was referred to me by another client. When she came in she was suffering from ovarian cancer. In the previous eighteen months she had been operated on twice for ovarian tumors, and twice they had grown back. Her appointment with me was on a Tuesday. She was due to go in for her third operation for ovarian cancer the following Tuesday.

When I met her it was apparent that she was the kind of person who disclosed very little. Her defenses were strong and she was emotionally distant. She was not the kind of person you naturally felt comfortable with. Beneath her stiff exterior it was obvious that she was scared and angry. Given her defensiveness I decided to proceed very gently and slowly with her. She wasn't ready to face the blocks in her system and I didn't want to risk making her more distant and defensive.

After an initial conversation I had her lie down on my table. I began by placing one hand under her tailbone and the other hand over her lower abdomen. The energy started flowing through me immediately. Some of Barbara's stress and anxiety soon dissipated and within a few minutes she nodded off. As I proceeded to work on her pelvic region the energy flowing into her became very strong and hot. I could hear lots of "popping" going on in the area around her ovaries. The "popping" sound continued until the session was over. At the end of the hour the energy diminished and Barbara woke up.

After she collected herself and got off the table I asked her to come in again on Friday because I wanted another opportunity to work on her before she went in for surgery the following Tuesday. She agreed. When she left she was feeling better.

Two days later, on Thursday morning, she called my office and cancelled her appointment for Friday. I asked her why. Her condition was serious. She told me she had never been as depressed as she was that morning and didn't want to come back in and get even more depressed. I told her that I understood it wasn't fun to be depressed but it also wasn't fun to have cancer. "Actually," I continued. "I know you feel very bad and you blame me for the depression you're feeling but I must tell you that what you're going through is very important. It tells me that you're discharging a lot of the depression and resentment that's been sitting in your system. I feel that negative energy has had a great deal to do with your cancer. Hopefully between now and Tuesday all that negativity will be completely discharged. If so, when the surgeon opens up that area one of two things could happen. Both are good. First, the surgeon will remove the remaining tumors. With luck they won't grow back because you will have gotten rid of the negative energy environment that fed the cancer. The second possibility is that the surgeon will open you up and there won't be any cancer left at all."

Our conversation concluded quickly after that. I wished her luck, and she thanked me for my help. A week later I received a call from the client who had referred Barbara to me. "Has Barbara called you?" she asked.

"No," I said.

"Well you won't believe this. She went in for surgery on Tuesday. When they opened her up there was nothing there. No cancer. Nothing. They sewed her up and sent her home."

Sometimes we get lucky and something lovely like that happens. In Barbara's case releasing the blocked negative energy in her pelvis allowed the cancer to dissolve. Going through a day of depression was a small price to pay for the healing she received.

# 11

Richard was a gifted Psychologist who had gone through a bitter divorce. When he came in to see me he had gained sixty pounds and contracted Chronic Fatigue Syndrome (CFS). While the marriage was legally over the emotional repercussions of what he had gone through during the divorce proceedings had served to keep much of the hostility alive in his psyche.

When we started our work together and the healing energy began flowing into him the first piece of unfinished business that came up from the depths of his unconscious surprisingly did not concern his marriage but his childhood. As he lay on the healing table he saw himself in his crib as an infant about a year old. He had wet his diaper and was crying because he was uncomfortable. After what seemed like a long time to him his mother came into the bedroom and instead of changing his diaper, beat him with a coat hanger. While in time he recovered from the physical beating, he never got over its emotional effect. The experience had been seared deeply into his soul. Because of its effect on his psyche he never allowed himself to get angry as an adult. Since he couldn't get angry, he was unable to set boundaries to protect himself and was also incapable of aligning himself with a higher power to augment his energy and find his wholeness. He had positioned himself perfectly in the victim role. Subconsciously, he had shut himself off at his core in the hope that he wouldn't be exposed and made vulnerable again. Although he didn't know it at the time all he was doing was enduring and surviving his life.

In a positive sense, his divorce had brought his powerlessness and victimization issues to the surface. His ex-wife had gone for his jugular. He had not fought back. Instead he had come down with CFS. As his childhood images flooded into his consciousness I directed him to connect to the traumatized feelings he had felt as a defenseless baby being beaten in his crib. It was a very difficult thing for him to do. There were many layers of psychic sediment between his conscious mind and where the trauma was buried in his body. Getting through them required a great deal of concentration. Finally, he began to feel a little of the terror. I asked him to give the terror a sound and make that sound as if it were coming from the part of his body where he felt it. After a few false starts he was soon screaming at the top of his lungs and all the bottled emotion that had been stuck in his system was finally released.

As the layer of terror subsided I had him go deeper into the trauma and find his rage. This request made him very uncomfortable. He didn't want to go there. I knew he must. Without finding his rage there would be no healing. We went round and round again for a little while, then he surrendered and touched the rage, making a little sound.

"That's good," I said. "Now do it again, only louder. Your mother's not here to punish you or threaten your life. You can get as angry a you want. No one will punish, threaten or disapprove of you. If you don't let your rage out I can't help you. No one can. So help yourself. It's time. It's up to you. Go for it."

With that he let out a huge roar and kept roaring for a long time. He kicked the table, flailed wildly with his arms and sweated copiously. When all the rage was out of his system he lay back on the table and rested for a few minutes.

As he lay there he told me a very interesting thing had happened to him on the table. While he had been expressing his rage he had seen faint tendrils of energy wrapped around the subtle energy centers, or chakras in his stomach and pelvis. As he continued to express his rage these tendrils of energy let go of their grip on his energy centers. He was certain these tendrils came from his ex-wife and that she had been stealing his energy unconsciously. When he got up off the table he was glowing like a Christmas tree. In the center of his chest a reddish brown circle appeared on his skin about two inches in diameter that hadn't been there when we began. He left feeling very light and happy.

The circle in the center of his chest was the result of his heart center opening. When he expressed his rage and released the tendrils that were stealing his life force it allowed the energy within his own system to move up to a higher octave and open his heart center. This type of opening is part of the vertical ascent.

Six months later when I returned to Austin Richard came to see me again. The CFS was gone, he had lost the sixty pounds he had gained, and he was building a successful practice helping many people.

Since then I have worked with many people who have contracted CFS. In every case that I have seen there was a common thread. The conditions that allowed CFS to manifest in all my clients' lives started very early in their life with another person, usually a parent, siphoning off or stealing their life force when they were very young and vulnerable. This pattern of energy stealth continued on for many years leading to the chronic depletion of their available energy, setting the stage for CFS to manifest in their adult years.

# 12

Isabelle was in her mid-fifties when she first came to see me. She had been suffering from depression all her life. We did a series of ten sessions together to address her problem. As we progressed more and more of her depressed energy kept coming up to the surface where it could be discharged. After each session she would feel tired and drained for a few days. Midway through the program she began to wonder if she might be getting worse instead of better and if all this work we were doing was simply a waste of time and money. I told her I would be concerned if she left feeling great after each session. That would mean nothing was happening of a transformative nature. The fact that she was feeling some degree of discomfort meant that the healing process was moving very quickly toward resolution.

Thankfully, by her tenth session all the depressed, heavy energy had been flushed from her system. All those layers had been cleared away. Now the healing energy was able to lift her higher on the vertical ascent, instead of bringing up her depression. She found herself floating in a bright white light, detached from her body. When the session was over she described what she had experienced. She had never felt so whole, happy and peaceful in her life.

A few weeks later she was given a promotion in her civil service rating at the military base where she worked. A pay raise of several thousand dollars per year accompanied the promotion. At that time, a promotion of the sort Isabelle received was unheard of. There was more to come. A short time later she was notified that she had won a national art competition in a major magazine. A cash prize of several thousand dollars accompanied her victory. She called me later to inform me of these events and to thank me for helping her because she knew there was a direct connection between her inner transformation and her material success. "I am reminded of the Lord's teaching," she said. "Seek Ye first the Kingdom of God and all else shall be added unto you. It has certainly been true in my case."

A few months later her son-in-law called from Los Angeles. He was a frustrated actor who couldn't find work. We arranged to do a session over the telephone. When he called I saw a large block in his heart. I asked him to talk to me about his father. As he did so I sent him the healing energy. His father was an alcoholic and a critical, emotionally distant parent. This young man had all sorts of pain and shame around his father and suffered from low self-esteem. As he talked on about his Dad I could tell that the energy block in his heart was now mobilized and ready to break. So I asked him how did it *feel* to have an alcoholic, shaming father. With that question the energy block broke wide open and all the pain, grief and heartbreak around his relationship to his father came to the surface. He cried and sobbed for the entire hour on the phone as I continued to send him the healing energy. By the end of the hour he was all cried out. I never spoke to him again but Isabelle, his mother-in-law, called me a few weeks later to report what had happened in his life as a result of the work we had done. In short order he had landed several major commercials that paid him handsomely. The negative beliefs he held about himself had been purged from his psyche and his reality had shifted upward as a result.

### The Beacon Program

When we walk through the T Zone the negative emotional content buried in our system comes up to be processed and discharged. If we can't feel our pain we won't be able to heal it. The good news is that the discomfort one might feel during the healing process is short term and short lived.

I've developed a program to take my clients through the T Zone and help them heal their lives. It's called The Beacon Program. The Beacon Program focuses on the long term. Long term is defined here as the rest of one's life. The purpose of The Beacon Program is to take clients to the next level of their life experience and evolution. The price one has to pay to walk through the T Zone pales in comparison with the benefits one receives for transforming his or her consciousness.

In designing The Beacon Program I have divided it into three levels: basic, intermediate and advanced. Each level consists of ten one hour healing sessions with me. Normally these sessions are scheduled once a week for ten weeks. Sometimes, depending upon a client's need The Beacon Program can be fitted into a shorter time period or stretched out to accommodate a longer period than ten weeks.

For clients living outside of Los Angeles (where I currently reside) The Beacon Program can be delivered over the telephone. The Program loses nothing in terms of its effectiveness and power when delivered by phone. The only difference is that phone clients don't see me in person. Sometimes that is an advantage because it means my inner sight will not be distracted by visual elements in the environment.

For many clients the basic level of The Beacon Program is sufficient. In ten sessions we can usually achieve a great deal. Other clients may want to go farther in the healing process, depending on their time, need and financial situation.

I have chosen ten sessions as the basic number of sessions needed to make a long-term impact in my client's lives. While it is true that many of the healing "tales from the T Zone" recounted in this chapter occurred in one session it is also true that these experiences consisted of healing one layer of trauma in a client's psyche. Ten sessions provides a significantly greater opportunity to heal more than one layer of traumatic material in the unconscious and make considerable progress in the vertical ascent.

While life is not fair the one thing we all have in common is some degree of consciousness and the potential for much more. What we do with that potential is up to us. If we develop our consciousness we increase the odds of having a significantly better life. The Beacon Program has been formulated to help those who are ready to work for more consciousness move forward in this most precious of life tasks. If you would like to participate in The Beacon Program you may contact us through the following venues:

> **by phone**   (310) 392-5105
>
> **by mail**   The Beacon Program
> 2340 Ashland Avenue
> Santa Monica, CA 90405
>
> **by e-mail**   beaconprogram@ibm.net